James Jacques J. Tissot

The Life of our Saviour Jesus Christ

three hundred and sixty-five compositions from the four Gospels - Vol. 3

James Jacques J. Tissot

The Life of our Saviour Jesus Christ
three hundred and sixty-five compositions from the four Gospels - Vol. 3

ISBN/EAN: 9783337314774

Printed in Europe, USA, Canada, Australia, Japan

Cover: Foto ©Lupo / pixelio.de

More available books at **www.hansebooks.com**

THE LIFE OF OUR SAVIOUR

JESVS CHRIST

THREE HUNDRED AND SIXTY-FIVE COMPOSITIONS
FROM THE FOUR GOSPELS
WITH NOTES AND EXPLANATORY DRAWINGS
BY
J. JAMES TISSOT
NOTES TRANSLATED BY Mrs ARTHUR BELL (N. D'ANVERS)

VOL. III.

O vos omnes qui transitis per viam, attendite et videte si est dolor sicut dolor meus.

O all ye that pass by behold and see if there be any sorrow like unto my sorrow.

Copyright 1895 by J. James Tissot.
Copyright 1896 by J. James Tissot.
Copyright 1899 by J. James Tissot.

All illustrations entered according to the Act of Congress, in the years 1895, 1896 and 1899, by
J. James Tissot, in the Office of the Librarian of Congress, at Washington.

HOLY WEEK

PREFACE

We have now reached an especially anxious period of the life of Jesus. It is not yet that of the grand dramas of the Passion, but it is their Prelude, and they are ushered in by an inquietude baffling description, such as is felt in the oppressive stillness heralding some grand convulsion of nature.

A vague murmur gradually begins to make itself heard, increasing as it gathers about the person of the Master. The very triumph of *Palm Sunday*, with which *Holy Week* opens, is not free from terror, for from the feverish fickleness of the crowd one cannot but feel that their enthusiasm has no real foundation; and, moreover, one foresees how this hour of triumph will weigh against Him in the balance with the enemies of the Lord, for it will be looked upon by them as a defiance.

When we recalled certain hours of the *Holy Childhood*, they presented, in spite of an occasional prophetic gloom, a series of quietly attractive scenes taking place in well-beloved, congenial surroundings, and combining all the poetry of ancient legend whilst retaining the stamp of truth.

Then, again, when we passed on to the *Ministry*, the subjects treated were set in a framework of Jewish life in which Jesus moved as a reformer, and which I felt bound to describe with considerable fulness. The active life led by Jesus gave me, moreover, an opportunity for traversing the whole of the deeply interesting and picturesque country which was the scene of His public career, and the characteristics of which are so well reflected in all their ideal simplicity in His discourses, interspersed as they are with parables and life-like metaphors. Now, however, when the hour of the last scene is approaching, it is about the Temple, the centre of a confused and menacing agitation, that the events of the Saviour's life are to group themselves.

In fact, to consummate this mission, Jesus had to approach the unique focus whence radiates, for the people of Israel, the whole of their religious life. There were to be struck the last grand blows: there was to be prepared the supreme catastrophe. A divine reformer, Jesus came to attack that jealous aristocracy which arrogated to its own profit a monopoly of all doctrinal influence. He would apparently be beaten in the conflict, but this defeat of a day would be the starting-point of a final victory, and the glory shed on His last hours by His presence in Jerusalem would mightily aid in the diffusion of the truth.

PREFACE

Jerusalem and the Temple were, therefore, what I had to represent in addition to the data peculiar to each separate scene. I have done my best, carefully rendering in several pictures the general aspect and internal organization of that citadel of the very spirit of Judaism with all its devotion to formalism and to the letter of the law.

I have, moreover, endeavoured to bring out the characteristic modification which the facts recorded appear to indicate as having taken place in the state of mind of Jesus Himself. No doubt that which He now willed, He had always willed, but He had not always manifested His will in the same manner. When He for the first time lends Himself to a popular demonstration; when He opens communications with the Gentiles; when, acting on His own authority alone, He cast out of the Temple those that bought and sold; when He openly predicted the destruction of the sacred edifice without which Jewish worship could no longer be carried on; when, lastly, He publicly attacked the sacerdotal caste, pitilessly scourging the hypocritical scribes and Pharisees and calling them a generation of vipers, does not His conduct seem to be instinct with an unusual audacity, which would appear to aim at precipitating events?

In His external appearance, also, a certain change has passed over Jesus. His personality now manifests itself under a different aspect, and I have endeavoured to bring this out in my work, by accentuating the sombre and mysterious purpose conveyed by His acts in the last period of His life.

I have endeavoured to show the toils gradually closing in around Him; the tragic fate approaching more and more nearly, and becoming inevitable in such a manner that the action of Judas, with which this portion of my work closes, and which connects it with the series of scenes to follow, should seem to the spectator to take place exactly at the right point for the *dénouement* of a situation which had become impossible, so that the approaching *Passion* had long been shadowed forth and explained beforehand.

By this means I have hoped to remain faithful to historic truth and to give a legitimate interpretation to the accounts of the Evangelists, which, as is well known, has been my chief aim throughout this work.

Capital from the El-Aksa Mosque

HOLY WEEK

THE FIRST FOUR DAYS

PALM SUNDAY

The Foal of Bethphage

Saint Matthew — Chap. 21

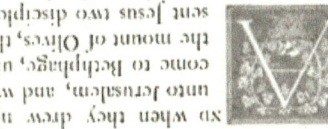

1 And when they drew nigh unto Jerusalem, and were come to Bethphage, unto the mount of Olives, then sent Jesus two disciples,

2. Saying unto them, Go into the village over against you, and straightway ye shall find an ass tied, and a colt with her: loose *them*, and bring *them* unto me.

3. And if any *man* say ought unto you, ye shall say, The Lord hath need of them; and straightway he will send them.

4. All this was done, that it might be fulfilled which was spoken by the prophet, saying,

5. Tell ye the daughter of Sion, Behold, thy King cometh unto thee, meek, and

1 Cum appropinquassent Jerosolymis et venissent Bethphage ad montem Oliveti, tunc Jesus misit duos discipulos,

2. Dicens eis: Ite in castellum, quod contra vos est, et statim invenietis asinam alligatam et pullum cum ea; solvite et adducite mihi.

3. Et si quis vobis aliquid dixerit, dicite, quia Dominus his opus habet, et confestim dimittet eos.

4. Hoc autem totum factum est, ut adimpleretur quod dictum est per prophetam dicentem:

5. Dicite filiæ Sion: Ecce Rex tuus venit tibi mansuetus, sedens super

HOLY WEEK

SANCT. MARC. — c. 11

4. Et abeuntes invenerunt pullum ligatum ante januam foris in bivio, et solvunt eum.

5. Et quidam de illic stantibus dicebant illis: Quid facitis solventes pullum?

6. Qui dixerunt eis sicut præceperat illis Jesus; et dimiserunt eis.

7. Et duxerunt pullum ad Jesum, et imponunt illi vestimenta sua, et sedit super eum.

asinam et pullum filium subjugalis.

SAINT MARK — CH. 11

4. And they went their way, and found the colt tied by the door without in a place where two ways met; and they loose him.

5. And certain of them that stood there said unto them, What do ye, loosing the colt?

6. And they said unto them even as Jesus had commanded: and they let them go.

7. And they brought the colt to Jesus, and cast their garments on him; and he sat upon him.

sitting upon an ass, and a colt the foal of an ass.

THE FOAL OF BETHPHAGE

SANCT. LUC. — c. 19

29. Et factum est, quum appropinquassct ad Bethphage et Bethaniam, ad montem, qui vocatur Oliveti, misit duos discipulos suos,

30. Dicens : Ite in castellum, quod contra est, in quod introeuntes invenietis pullum asinæ alligatum, cui nemo unquam hominum sedit; solvite illum et adducite.

31. Et si quis vos interrogaverit : Quare solvitis? sic dicetis ei : Quia Dominus operam ejus desiderat.

32. Abierunt autem qui missi erant, et invenerunt, sicut dixit illis, stantem pullum.

33. Solventibus autem illis pullum, dixerunt domini ejus ad illos : Quid solvitis pullum?

SAINT LUKE. — CHAP. 19

29. And it came to pass, when he was come nigh to Bethphage and Bethany, at the mountcalled the mount of Olives, he sent two of his disciples,

30. Saying, Go ye into the village over against you, in the which at your entering ye shall find a colt tied, whereon yet never man sat : loose him, and bring him hither.

31. And if any man ask you, Why do ye loose him? thus shall ye say unto him, Because the Lord hath need of him.

32. And they that were sent went their way, and found even as he had said unto them.

33. And as they were loosing the colt, the owners thereof said unto them, Why loose ye the colt?

The Procession on the Mount of Olives.

HOLY WEEK

34. At illi dixerunt : Quia Dominus cum necessarium habet.

35. Et duxerunt illum ad Jesum, et jactantes vestimenta sua supra pullum, imposuerunt Jesum.

34. And they said, The Lord hath need of him.

35. And they brought him to Jesus : and they cast their garments upon the colt, and they set Jesus thereon.

To imitate Bethphage the Latin text of Saint Matthew uses the word castellum, which would imply a village with its castle or tower of defence. In fact, the sanctuary of Bethphage, which has now been tenantly marked the spot where Jesus mounted the colt, is situated at the base of a mount, the summit of which is covered with very numerous fragments of pottery, a characteristic particularity of sites formerly inhabited. Moreover, this lofty spot above Bethany, from which can be seen the declivities sloping down to the Dead Sea, with the valley leading to Jericho and to Bethlehem, with all the districts on the south of Jerusalem, must, in view of its remarkable position, have constituted an important strategic point. It must, in fact, have been a stronghold of war; hence the choice of the name of castellum to designate the village of Bethphage.

We are completely in the dark as to which disciples were chosen to go and fetch the ass and her foal to Bethphage; all manner of conjectures have been hazarded, but not one with any foundation in fact. All we know is that the Master's instructions with regard to them were very precise: he was anxious to spare his messengers all difficulty, and told them what they were to answer in the very probable event of the owner of the two

The Procession of the Apostles.

animals protesting against their being taken. "Say ye that the Lord hath need of them," words which very clearly indicate the character of Jesus intended to give to His triumphal entrance into Jerusalem. He is the Lord Who has a right of ownership in all the possessions of man and the exercises this right with discretion.

It is noteworthy that on comparing the text of the various Evangelists, we find there of them. Saint Mark, Saint Luke and Saint John speaking of a colt only, whilst Saint Matthew mentions an ass and a colt. The words of Saint Luke, however, in chap. 19, verse 30, put us on the track of a perfectly natural explanation. The colt had never yet been mounted, and, therefore, there might be some fear that it would be restive, so they took its mother with it. Still Saint Matthew certainly expresses himself rather strangely in this matter, for he says : " And they brought the ass and the colt and put on them their clothes and they set him thereon." (In which the two does Saint Matthew mean that the Lord was set? On their clothes on one of the two animals, or first on one and then on the other? After what we have just said, the latter hypothesis is not tenable; but, then, why should the garments have been put on both? And, moreover,

The Procession on the Mount of Olives

Saint Luke – Chap. 19

E t cum appropinquaret jam ad descensum montis Oliveti, coeperunt omnes turbæ discipulorum gaudentes laudare Deum voce magna super omnibus, quas viderant, virtutibus;

38. Dicentes: Benedictus, qui venit rex in nomine Domini; pax in cœlo et gloria in excelsis.

39. Et quidam Pharisæorum de turbis dixerunt ad illum : Magister, increpa discipulos tuos.

40. Quibus ipse ait: Dico vobis, quia hi si tacuerint, lapides clamabunt.

SANCT. MATTH. — C. 21

8. Plurima autem turba straverunt vestimenta sua in via; alii autem cedebant ramos de arboribus et sternebant in via.

A ND when he was come nigh, even now at the descent of the Mount of Olives, the whole multitude of the disciples began to rejoice and praise God with a loud voice for all the mighty works that they had seen;

38. Saying, Blessed *be* the King that cometh in the name of the Lord : peace in heaven, and glory in the highest.

39. And some of the Pharisees from among the multitude said unto him, Master, rebuke thy disciples.

40. And he answered and said unto them, I tell you that, if these should hold their peace, the stones would immediately cry out.

SAINT MATTHEW — CH. 21

8. And a very great multitude spread their garments in the way; others cut down branches from the trees, and strawed *them* in the way.

Path on the Mount of Olives.

---

what a singular mode of expression is that of Saint Matthew. Strauss thinks it a good opportunity for holding the Evangelist up to ridicule, claiming that he made Jesus Christ ride on two animals at once, whereas the difficulty is really of the slightest, admitting of three or four quite acceptable explanations.

Jesus wept
Saint Luke — Chap. 19

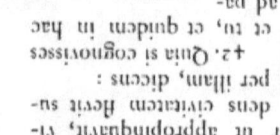

ut appropinquaret, videns civitatem flevit super illam, dicens:

42. Quia si cognovisses et tu, et quidem in hac die tua, quæ ad pacem tibi; nunc autem abscondita sunt ab oculis tuis.

43. Quia venient dies in te, et circumdabunt te inimici tui vallo, et circumdabunt te, et coangustabunt te undique,

44. Et ad terram prosternent te et filios tuos, qui in te sunt, et non relinquent in te lapidem super lapidem, eo quod non cognoveris tempus visitationis tuæ.

9. Turbæ autem, quæ præcedebant et quæ sequebantur, clamabant, dicentes: Hosanna filio David, benedictus qui venit in nomine Domini, hosanna in altissimis.

xix when he was come near, he beheld the city, and wept over it,

42. Saying, If thou hadst known, even thou, at least in this thy day, the things which belong unto thy peace! but now they are hid from thine eyes.

43. For the days shall come upon thee, that thine enemies shall cast a trench about thee, and compass thee round, and keep thee in on every side,

44. And shall lay thee even with the ground, and thy children within thee; and they shall not leave in thee one stone upon another; because thou knewest not the time of thy visitation.

9. And the multitudes that went before, and that followed, cried, saying, Hosanna to the son of David : Blessed is he that cometh in the name of the Lord; Hosanna in the highest.

The Procession in the Streets of Jerusalem

Saint Matthew — Chap. 21

 T quum intrasset Jerosolymam, commota est universa civitas, dicens : Quis est hic?

11. Populi autem dicebant : Hic est Jesus propheta a Nazareth Galilææ.

 ND when he was come into Jerusalem, all the city was moved, saying, Who is this?

11. And the multitude said, This is Jesus the prophet of Nazareth of Galilee.

The Procession in the Streets of Jerusalem.

The streets of Jerusalem are nearly all steep, being built along the flanks of the town hills on which the town is situated. These hills have been worked as quarries from the very earliest times, first for the construction of the Temple and then for the walls surrounding the suburbs round about Mount Sion and Mount Moriah. Portherefrom palaces erected between the time of David and that of Herod, whatever built with great tastiness, so made that these same quarries were drawn upon, so that beneath the courts of the Temple, and indeed, under the whole of the town of Jerusalem, are vast subterranean spaces, which may be said to bear a distant resemblance to the catacombs of Paris. All these underground vaults and passages were utilized in

times of war and also during the visitings so frequent at Jerusalem during the latter days. At the present day the only caves that can be identified are those known as the Tombs of the Kings, the entrance to which is near the Gate of Damascus; but that the other quarters of the town also had their subterranean grottoes has been abundantly proved in the course of the excavations necessitated by all the rebuilding which has been going on.

The Mishna tells us that Jewish women retired to caves beneath the Temple for the birth of their children, and that the little ones born in them were brought up in these retreats until they were seven, or, according to other accounts, even thirteen years old.

HOLY WEEK

The custom had originated in memory of the Captivity in Egypt, during the beginning of which the women of Israel used to withdraw for their confinement to the Desert, in the hope of saving their offspring from death; but the Egyptians having noticed this, the mothers resorted to hiding their babies in subterranean refuges. In commemoration of this fact, and of the wonderful way in which the children thus hidden throve under the direct protection of God, it became usual to dedicate a certain number of the boys, brought up as described above, to the service of the Temple. They appeared at the various ceremonies, contributing by their presence to the éclat of the services.

The soil of Jerusalem is at the present time far loftier than it was in former days, and the reason is not far to seek. Ever since its early days as a stronghold of the Jebusites that Kitosay for some

Sub-buildings of the Armenian Convent at Jerusalem.

three thousand years, materials of every description, with the necessary provisions of all manner of kinds for its inhabitants, have been pouring in whilst nothing has ever been taken out again, with the result that perfect mountains of filth and rubbish have been piled up here and there, serving as a foundation for the later buildings. These hills grew, in fact, to such a height, especially after the sieges and sackings to which the Holy City was subjected, that they are now loftier than the walls. And, on the side known as the Jewish quarter, they project beyond it and eject their surplus rubbish upon the slopes of Ophel.

Capital from the El-Aksa Mosque.

The Multitude in the Temple

THE CHILDREN CRYING HOSANNA!

Saint Matthew — Chap. 21

AND Jesus went into the temple of God,

15. And when the chief priests and scribes saw the wonderful things that he did, and the children crying in the temple, and saying, Hosanna to the son of David; they were sore displeased,

16. And said unto him, Hearest thou what these say? And Jesus saith unto them, Yea; have ye never read, Out of the mouth of babes and sucklings thou hast perfected praise?

Temple. This Porch or gallery, which had recently been completed by Herod, consisted of five naves formed by four rows of Corinthian columns; there were one hundred and sixty of these columns, and in the centre, on both the Royal Porch were four thicker columns which four men together were scarcely able to encircle with their arms. This part of the Temple was shady throughout the day, and was, therefore, much resorted to by the people; the Pharisees preferred it as did the Sadducees and other sects, each of which had its doctors

'r intravit Jesus in templum Dei...

15. Videntes autem principes sacerdotum et scribæ mirabilia quæ fecit, et pueros clamantes in templo et dicentes : Hosanna filio David, indignati sunt

16. Et dixerunt ei : Audis quid isti dicunt? Jesus autem dixit eis : Utique; numquam legistis : Quia ex ore infantium et lactentium perfecisti laudem?

The Temple was entered from the right and worship persued on at again on the left. The circulation of the Temple being from west to east, the right half of it was on the south and the left on the north. It was, therefore, possible to go in by the door at the north-west angle and leave again by that on the north-east corner, after having gone twice round the Temple. To reach it from the location, therefore, Jesus must necessarily have passed over the so-called Xystus Bridge on to which opened the Royal Porch on the south of the

Vicinities of Jerusalem.

and its preachers who drew around them a crowd of adepts. It was, moreover, a convenient spot for watching what was going on in the Court of the Gentiles, a considerable portion of which is situated between the Royal Porch and the balustrade of the Chel, or the little rampart, already described, surrounding, as we have explained, the buildings of the actual Temple. Here might be seen this or that celebrity, this or that fashionable doctor or teacher surrounded by his disciples, the crowd of lookers-on gathering wherever the interest of the moment happened to be concentrated.

The Porch most frequented after that called by the Greeks the Xoos Basilica was the one named after Solomon, for which Jesus seemed to have a special affection. It was situated, as is well known, on the east of the Temple in front of the Nicanor Gate; it had two rows of columns, so that there was some shade to be found in it, especially in the morning until noon. It would, therefore, be in these two portions of the sacred building that the crowds would gather; the children brought up and employed in the Temple would join them and the multitude would be swelled by all the strangers who came to admire the new buildings and to worship in them in accordance with the requirements of the law.

HOLY WEEK

MONDAY

The Chief Priests take counsel together
TO DESTROY JESUS
Saint Mark – Chap. 11, v. 18

The Chief Priests take counsel together.

ET audito principes sacerdotum et scribæ quærebant quomodo eum perderent; timebant enim eum, quoniam universa turba admirabatur super doctrina ejus.

AND the scribes and chief priests heard it, and sought how they might destroy him: for they feared him, because all the people was astonished at his doctrine.

The triumphal procession had passed by quiet and had been restored to the Royal Porch, for the crowd had gone after Jesus, and none were left but a few groups of the usual frequenters.

HOLY WEEK

of the colonnades, such as the doctors and their attendants of various sects, amongst whom Pharisees predominated. It was easy enough for them to convince themselves of the growing importance of the Nazarene, for things, and indeed, fresh sounds of excitement reached them from the town and its environs every moment, confirming the signification of the events of which they had all just been witnesses. There was no doubt that the resurrection of Lazarus had forcibly appealed to the imagination of all, kindling the hopes of everyone, so that the official authorities were beginning to find themselves at the mercy of every caprice of the new Prophet. Now, from the first He had shewn little favour to the Pharisees, and they might, therefore, well fear that He would not hesitate to make a dead set against their influence. There was, then, no time to be lost: they must have done with this man. The secret meeting in the house of Caiaphas was known, its probable results were commented on, and what would be the best measures to take to counteract this increase of popular favour were eagerly discussed. As for Jesus Himself, all He did on that day was to pass through the Temple, which He entered from the town and left by the Susa Gate, which was later, notably in the time of the Saracens, overtly called the Golden Gate. Then, traversing the Valley of Jehoshaphat, He was able, by climbing obliquely the Mount of Olives, to make His way to Bethany, where, no doubt, He lived until the following Thursday. However that may be, we shall leave Him no more, and the Gospel will give us details as numerous as they are precious on this last period of His life on earth. It will shew Him going to the Temple sometimes before daybreak, spending long hours there, and only returning home at nightfall. It will explain to us every act of His, however apparently trivial, in every hour, nay every minute; enable us to listen to His discourses; will invite us to receive His supreme admonitions, given in the addresses which became ever more and more frequent. In a word, the Gospel will initiate us into all the mystery of those last days which were to end with the greatest event in the history of the human race.

Members of the Tribunal

15

The accursed Fig-tree
Saint Matthew — Chap. 21

ane autem revertens in civitatem esuriit.

19. Et videns fici arborem unam secus viam venit ad eam, et nihil invenit in ea nisi folia tantum, et ait illi : Numquam ex te fructus nascatur in sempiternum. Et arefacta est continuo ficulnea.

20. Et videntes discipuli mirati sunt, dicentes : Quomodo continuo aruit?

21. Respondens autem Jesus ait eis: Amen dico vobis, si habueritis fidem et non hæsitaveritis, non solum de ficulnea facietis, sed et si monti huic dixeritis: Tolle et jacta te in mare, fiet.

22. Et omnia quæcumque petieritis in oratione credentes, accipietis.

ow in the morning as he returned into the city, he hungered.

19. And when he saw a fig-tree in the way, he came to it, and found nothing thereon, but leaves only, and said unto it, Let no fruit grow on thee henceforward for ever. And presently the fig-tree withered away.

20. And when the disciples saw *it*, they marvelled, saying, How soon is the fig-tree withered away!

21. Jesus answered and said unto them, Verily I say unto you, If ye have faith, and doubt not, ye shall not only do this *which is done* to the fig-tree, but also if ye shall say unto this mountain, Be thou removed, and be thou cast into the sea; it shall be done.

22. And all things, whatsoever ye shall ask in prayer, believing, ye shall receive.

A Fig-tree in the Valley of Hinnom.

Judæa is the land of the fig-tree, and throughout the whole year its foliage beautifies the lower districts of the valleys near the springs and watercourses. On the slopes of the mountains

The accursed Fig-tree.

too, the fig-trees make patches of shade in the fields of wheat and barley, and even on the mountain tops they occur amongst the olives, to bear witness to the ownership of man and to the wealth of cultivation throughout the entire country. Travellers recognize three varieties of the fig-tree in Judæa, and these three are also referred to in the Talmud. First, there are the black or white figs, which are ripe in the month of June; then, the summer figs, which ripen in August, and it was doubtless beneath a tree of this second kind, during the time of vintage, that Jesus first saw Nathanael, when one look from Him changed his very soul. Lastly, there are the long-shaped violet figs which remain on the trees all the winter and are not gathered till the spring. Most of these trees, if they are sheltered from the wind, retain their foliage throughout the bad season unless the winter should be unusually severe, and the fig-tree of Egypt, thanks to the exceptional climate of the Delta, and the constant humidity of the soil, sometimes yields seven crops in one year.

Christ driving out them that sold in the Temple.

Christ driving out them that sold in the Temple
Saint Matthew – Chap. 21

T intravit Jesus in templum Dei, et ejiciebat omnes vendentes et ementes in templo, et mensas numulariorum et cathedras vendentium columbas evertit,

13. Et dicit eis: Scriptum est: Domus mea domus orationis vocabitur; vos autem fecistis illam speluncam latronum.

ND Jesus went into the temple of God, and cast out all them that sold and bought in the temple, and overthrew the tables of the moneychangers, and the seats of them that sold doves,

13. And said unto them, It is written, My house shall be called the house of prayer; but ye have made it a den of thieves.

We have already said a few words on the circumstances which led to this action of Jesus, an action apparently violent, but in reality quite natural. Between Solomon's Porch and the outer wall of the Temple on the eastern side, there was a certain space set apart for the animals to be offered up in sacrifice. It was from this space, after a first selection had been made, that they were taken to the Priests whose duty it was to examine them carefully according to rigidly prescribed rules, when they were led to the sheep-pool to be purified. In the space above referred to, which was a kind of long narrow passage, there were beneath the portico a number of little vaulted rooms resembling the shops in a bazaar, where congregated the buyers, money-changers and merchants. The premises, however, soon became too small, and the traders in animals gradually encroached on the other portions of the Temple. To begin with, the money-changers, going up a few steps, took their stand on the right and left of Solomon's Porch, others imitated their example, and soon the entire colonnade was invaded, especially at the time of the great festivals. Nor did the abuse end there; even the Court of the Gentiles was in its turn invaded and defiled by the animals bought and sold in it. Now, this court was paved with large polished stones with a slope managed, as already explained, so as to receive rain water and conduct it to the cisterns. The water in the cisterns of the Temple must, therefore, have been contaminated by impurities, whilst the silence of the sacred precincts was broken by all the confused noises of the market. Preaching, prayer and quiet meditation were all alike impossible; the state of things was scandalous; no one could now retire to the cool shade of the Temple in the morning, for it was then that the traffic was at its height. Everyone realized the abuses resulting from the deplorable invasion; but no one had the courage to take the initiative in trying to put a stop to it. Jesus alone, with the authority which

Jewish children.

radiated forth from His personality, could have hoped to bring such an attempt to a successful issue. He took off a kind of girdle, made of rope, which He wore round His robes, twisted it into a sort of scourge and used it as a whip to drive out them that sold. Behind Him in procession followed His disciples who, amidst great confusion, gradually cleared out the purchasers, till the portico was restored to its original tranquillity.

There can be no doubt that everybody except the merchants themselves, who were thus unceremoniously hustled out with their goods and chattels, was very glad of this successful measure of repression; the people could not fail to appreciate the fact that the healthiness of the Temple had gained greatly in every way; whilst the cleansing of the porticoes and their restoration to tranquillity were of paramount importance to them as the spots sacred to religious worship. Moreover, the purification of the waters of the cisterns; the restoration of the place set apart for the teaching of the prophets; the return of sanctity to the holy spot; in a word, everything combined to make the intervention of Jesus peculiarly opportune. The High Priests alone, the exalted officials of the Jewish nation, on whom had devolved the right of organizing the police of the Temple, were hurt at the initiative being thus taken out of their hands, feeling that it was of the nature of a reproach to them. This view will come out clearly presently when they will go in a body to seek Jesus and

*demand of Him « by what authority doest Thou these things and who gave Thee this authority? »
Furious as they already were at the ever-growing influence of Jesus, they could not pardon
Him for an act of authority of such signal impressiveness and in such direct opposition to
what they looked upon as their own rights.*

Jesus forbids the carrying of vessels through the Temple
Saint Mark — Chap. 11, v. 16

 r non sinebat ut quisquam transferret vas per templum.

 nd would not suffer that any man should carry any vessel through the temple.

*Jesus, having undertaken to restore order in the House of His Father, did not content
Himself with the first sweeping reform just described. Yet another abuse had crept in : namely,
the crossing of the Temple with various vessels in which
to fetch water more conveniently than by going round.
To understand more clearly how this custom came to be
introduced, what has already been said about the system
of the water supply of Jerusalem must be borne in
mind. We know, indeed we have just repeated, that all
those portions of the Temple open to the sky were paved
with polished stones and, in some parts, with many co-
loured marbles intended to receive rain water and take it
to the cisterns or reservoirs. These reservoirs were numerous, and were much frequented by the women of the
town, who flocked to them to draw water for their domes-
tic needs. Besides rain water these reservoirs received
the water from the sealed fountain on the further side
of Bethlehem and Etam, beyond the Wâdy Urtas. The
water from Solomon's Pools was also diverted to them
by means of the aqueducts already referred to. The reservoirs thus fed were celebrated, and their water was
much sought after on account of its freshness and purity;
the people, however, preferred to draw it from the cisterns adjoining the Temple to going to fetch it from
outside the town at Amygdalum or in the reservoirs of
the Valley of Gihon. This was the cause of the perpetual*

Women of Geba, Samaria.

*going and coming which destroyed the retirement of the Temple. It was not, however, the only one,
for all those who wished to go to any place beyond the Temple preferred taking a short cut
through it to going round the whole of the vast enceinte, which would have needed a very
wide détour.*

The same kind of thing may often be seen in Italy, in the Duomo of Florence, for instance, where bakers, porters and workmen pursuing their various avocations cross the sacred building to avoid going round by the road and to enjoy being in the shade for a moment or two. But Jesus could not bear to look on at such an abuse; He therefore forbade everyone to cross the Temple carrying loads, so as to restore to the consecrated spot the quiet and seclusion which rightly belonged to it.

At the present day it is still forbidden to cross the Haram, as the site of the Temple is now called, but the Pasha of Jerusalem has made an exception in favour of the sisters of Saint Vincent de Paul, for he is full of admiration for the charitable zeal which leads them to go from hospital to hospital throughout the town, ministering without distinction to all sufferers whether Christian or Mahommedan.

The Healing of the Lame in the Temple
Saint Matthew — Chap. 21, verse 14

T accesserunt ad eum cæci et claudi in templo, et sanavit eos.

ND the blind and the lame came to him in the temple; and he healed them.

The scene referred to in the Gospel must have taken place in the Court of the Women about seven o'clock in the morning, beyond the shade where the crowd is massed in my picture.

There could have been none but Jews present, for to reach this court it was necessary to pass through the Chel or terrace surrounding the actual buildings of the Temple to which, as is well

The Healing of the Lame in the Temple.

known, Gentiles were not admitted. The Temple at this early hour is full of the poor; the rich with their wide phylacteries and their gorgeous fringes will arrive later. In the distance can be seen the semi-circular steps of the Degrees, or Psalms, at the base of which devotees danced with torches in their hands at the ceremony of water-pouring at the Feast of Tabernacles. Originally this Festival was celebrated by a mere procession; but later, with a view to making it more impressive, specially decorated torches were introduced, and, as with all such customs, abuses gradually crept in. The Talmud refers to certain eccentricities of behaviour which drew considerable attention on those who practised them. Ben Jocades, for instance, boasted of the extraordinary leaps he took at the celebrations of festivals. We are also told that Ben Simon ben Lakist danced whilst juggling eight golden torches at once without letting them touch each other or dropping a single one. He bent his knees, linked his thumbs together, turned a somersault, and with a rebound stood once more upright, which reads, as will strike everyone, like a description of some modern acrobat's dangerous feats. In these festivals, moreover, if we are to believe the Talmudic accounts, there were singers who did wonderful things with their voices; a certain Higros, we are told, had an immense variety of melodies in his repertory, and, by putting his thumb in his mouth as he sung, he produced such extraordinary modulations of sound, that his brother Priests held their heads in both hands in their astonishment. This *may be quoted as an example of the silly, futile way in which the people exaggerated, giving to the slightest detail an undue importance which in the end acquired the force of a law.*

Jesus goes out to Bethany in the evening
Saint Mark — Chap. 11, verse 11

r circumspectis omnibus, quum jam vespera esset hora, exiit in Bethaniam cum duodecim.

nd when he had looked round about upon all things, and now the eventide was come, he went out unto Bethany with the twelve.

The day had been a very full one for Jesus and, as the Evangelist tells us, « He had looked round about upon all things ». He had taken care for everyone. He had put everything in order, making Himself alike a providence for the poor and a terror to the sinful merchants. But now that the eventide had come and the crowd had quitted the Temple, the Lord, accompanied by the twelve Apostles, who followed Him at a distance down the slopes of the Mount of Olives, set forth on His return to Bethany. After passing through one of the two gates of the Temple on the north-east side, they left the town by the Sheep-gate, then, going down the Valley of Jehoshaphat, they would reach at its lower extremity a spot full of tombs of some importance hewn in the rock. There, at the base of the Mount of Olives, were gardens with caves to which Jesus often resorted with His disciples. These gardens belonged to different owners, and in one of them was an oil-press called Gethsemane, belonging to one of the friends of Our Lord. Crossing the bridge over the brook Kedron, generally dried up at that spot, a road was reached, overshadowed by great pine-trees full of doves, and beneath the shade of which were shops, frequented by those who wished to buy suitable offerings for the Temple. After skirting along the gardens the travellers crossed the slopes of the Mount of Olives by a path leading also to the summit of the neighbouring Mount Scopus,

Path from Gethsemane to the Mount of the Ascension.

where Titus established his camp when he besieged Jerusalem. This same Mount Scopus was reserved during the Feast of Pentecost as a resting-place for the people of Galilee, and it was on this account, no doubt, that Jesus chose this route, reaching Bethphage first, and going

JESUS GOES OUT TO BETHANY IN THE EVENING

Jesus goes out to Bethany in the evening.

from thence to Bethany, which was on the right, about half an hour's walk farther on.

It was by this route, also, that the venerable David made his way to the desert weeping, with his head covered and his feet bare as he fled before his son Absalom, who had usurped his throne. Once arrived at the summit of the Mount of Olives, the traveller turning round had the whole of the Valley of Jehoshaphat spread out beneath him, that valley already shrouded in the shadows of the eventide, with the grand walls of the Temple beyond dominating the whole scene. From this point could be made out all the most important portions of the superb structure, with the enceinte of the Temple itself, the walls encircling it, the massive supplementary buildings dedicated to various purposes, whilst on the right, rising above everything else, were the towers of the Antonia Citadel. It was in this citadel that the Roman troops were stationed, and now and then could be heard the shrill blasts of their trumpets, breaking for a moment into the silence of the evening only to render it all the more solemn when the sound died away again. The groups of buildings were succeeded by a vacant space known as the Tyropœan valley, beyond which again rose the rest of the town, extending to Herod's Palace situated on Mount Zion, which formed the culminating point of the city. Farther away were the western slopes behind which the sun was setting; Jerusalem, with her back turned towards the light, seeming to wrap herself in a shroud of darkness before sinking to sleep.

All was calm, the west wind from the Mediterranean sweeping in its passage over the surface of the calcareous rocks baked through and through with the heat of the day's sunshine, brought to the eastern district where Jesus was walking an atmosphere still hot and laden with the scent of the incense which had recently been offered up in sacrifice. The number of substances used in making this incense and the very strong odour it emitted are well known, and we have already related some of the curious details on the subject given in the Talmud. In fine weather, and with a favourable wind, the column of scented air which went up from the Temple services would be dispersed all over the country; under certain conditions reaching even to the Jordan.

TUESDAY
The Gentiles ask to see Jesus
Saint John – Chap. 12

ERANT autem quidam Gentiles ex his, qui ascenderant, ut adorarent in die festo.

21. Hi ergo accesserunt ad Philippum, qui erat a Bethsaida Galilææ, et rogabant eum dicentes : Domine, volumus Jesum videre.

22. Venit Philippus et dicit Andreæ, Andreas rursum et Philippus dixerunt Jesu.

23. Jesus autem respondit eis dicens : Venit hora, ut clarificetur Filius hominis.

24. Amen amen dico vobis, nisi granum frumenti cadens in terram mortuum fuerit,

25. Ipsum solum manet; si autem mortuum fuerit, multum fructum affert.

ND there were certain Greeks among them that came up to worship at the feast :

21. The same came therefore to Philip, which was of Bethsaida of Galilee, and desired him, saying, Sir, we would see Jesus.

22. Philip cometh and telleth Andrew : and again Andrew and Philip tell Jesus.

23. And Jesus answered them, saying, The hour is come, that the Son of man should be glorified.

24. Verily, verily, I say unto you, Except a corn of wheat fall into the ground and die, it abideth alone : but if it die, it bringeth forth much fruit.

A typical Jew of Jerusalem.

Of the three approaches to the Temple open to those who came from the town, the most remarkable and at the same time the most modern was that which, spanning the Tyropœon valley on the south-west, led across a bridge of three arches abutting on the Mount Zion side on the remains of the ancient Millo bastions near the Xystus porticoes, and on the other side on the Royal Porch or Naos Basilica, built by Herod some thirty years previously. It was

The Gentiles ask to see Jesus.

at this point that the Tyropœon valley, or the valley of cheeses, was deepest. There seems to be no doubt that it was by this, the grandest of all the approaches, that the Gentiles arrived who came to the Temple asking to see Jesus. From it, in the shade of the Naos Basilica and through the forest formed by the seventy-two columns, the outlines of all the buildings of the Temple would rise up before them, glowing in the midday sunlight. What has now become of these seventy-two Corinthian columns? After the taking of Jerusalem by Titus and the burning of the Temple, the cedar beams of the roof were consumed in the flames, whilst the columns fell and were most of them broken. It was the same with the four hundred other columns which upheld the roofs of the various courts. All these masses of stone and other débris remained where they had fallen, and, to drive away the Jews and the newly-made converts to Christianity, the Roman governors ordered all the filth and rubbish of the town to be thrown upon the ruins, so that a regular mountain soon rose up upon the site of the Temple. The Empress Helena, the mother of Constantine, was the first to begin to clear away the heaps of refuse; Justinian carried on her work and, for the building of the various sanctuaries which were now simultaneously erected in the Holy Land, the remains of the Temple were utilized. The best were reserved for the Basilica of the Nativity at Bethlehem and the Church of the Holy Sepulchre at Jerusalem, whilst that which later became the El-Aksa Mosque came next and was succeeded by others. This is why capitals exactly resembling each other are found alike in the Church of the Holy Sepulchre and in the El-Aksa and Es-Sakhra Mosques, which are on what was once the esplanade of the Temple. The same workmanship can be recognized in all the remains, proving beyond a doubt the identity of their origin.

The strangers who came to the Temple to see Jesus were probably from Cyprus. Out of respect for the Master, they were not likely to address Him directly, but probably preferred their request through Philip.

The Voice from Heaven
Saint John – Chap. 12

unc anima mea turbata est. Et quid dicam? Pater, salvifica me ex hac hora. Sed propterea veni in horam hanc.

28. Pater, clarifica nomen tuum. Venit ergo vox de cœlo: Et clarificavi et iterum clarificabo.

29. Turba ergo, quæ stabat et audierat, dicebat tonitruum esse factum. Alii dicebant: Angelus ei locutus est.

30. Respondit Jesus et dixit: Non propter me hæc vox venit, sed propter vos.

31. Nunc judicium est mundi, nunc princeps hujus mundi ejicietur foras.

32. Et ego si exaltatus fuero a terra, omnia traham ad me ipsum.

33. Hoc autem dicebat, significans qua morte esset moriturus.

34. Respondit ei turba: Nos audivimus ex lege, quia Christus manet in æternum, et quomodo tu dicis: Oportet

ow is my soul troubled, and what shall I say; Father, save me from this hour: but for this cause came I unto this hour.

28. Father, glorify thy name. Then came there a voice from heaven, *saying* I have both glorified *it*, and will glorify *it* again.

Site of the Court of the Gentiles: Haram. Mount Zion in the distance.

29. The people therefore, that stood by, and heard *it*, said that it thundered: others said, An angel spake to him.

30. Jesus answered and said, This voice came not because of me, but for your sakes.

31. Now is the judgment of this world: now shall the prince of this world be cast out.

32. And I, if I be lifted up from the earth, will draw all *men* unto me.

33. This he said, signifying what death he should die.

34. The people answered him, We have heard out of the law that Christ abideth for ever: and how sayest thou

THE VOICE FROM HEAVEN

exaltari Filium hominis? quis est iste Filius hominis?

35. Dixit ergo eis Jesus: Adhuc modicum lumen in vobis est. Ambulate, dum lucem habetis, ut non vos tenebræ comprehendant, et qui ambulat in tenebris, nescit quo vadat.

36. Dum lucem habetis, credite in lucem, ut filii lucis sitis. Hæc locutus est Jesus, et abiit et abscondit se ab eis.

37. Quum autem tanta signa fecisset coram eis, non credebant in eum.

38. Ut sermo Isaiæ prophetæ impleretur, quem dixit: Domine, quis credidit auditui nostro? et brachium Domini cui revelatum est?...

41. Hæc dixit Isaias, quando vidit gloriam ejus, et locutus est de eo.

42. Verumtamen et ex principibus multi crediderunt in eum; sed propter Pharisæos non confitebantur, ut a synagoga non ejicerentur;

The Son of man must be lifted up? who is this Son of man?

35. Then Jesus said unto them, Yet a little while is the light with you. Walk while ye have the light, lest darkness come upon you: for he that walketh in darkness knoweth not whither he goeth.

36. While ye have light, believe in the light, that ye may be the children of light. These things spake Jesus, and departed, and did hide himself from them.

37. But though he had done so many miracles before them, yet they believed not on him:

38. That the saying of Esaias the prophet might be fulfilled, which he spake, Lord, who hath believed our report? and to whom hath the arm of the Lord been revealed?

41. These things said Esaias, when he saw his glory, and spake of him.

42. Nevertheless among the chief rulers also many believed on him; but because of the Pharisees they did not confess *him*, lest they should be put out of the synagogue:

Young girls of Bethlehem.

43. Dilexerunt enim gloriam hominum magis quam gloriam Dei.	43. For they loved the praise of men more than the praise of God.

The Voice from Heaven.

In my picture Jesus is seen standing on the Chel, which was, as is well known, a terrace approached by twelve steps surrounding the sacred buildings in the enceinte of the Temple. It was from 4 to 5 yards wide and the Gentiles were forbidden to set foot on it under pain of death, as announced in inscriptions on the stones already referred to, set up at regular intervals and rising above the ornate balustrade protecting it. Those on this terrace could look down into the Court of the Gentiles, the largest of the various Temple Courts, and all the people there assembled were witnesses of the extraordinary miracle related in the Gospel. Judging from the comment made by the author of the sacred text, to the effect that some that stood by and heard it said that it thundered, we are, we think, justified in supposing that the sky was overcast as if threatening a storm. We see, however, from the words of Jesus Himself, as quoted in the text, that He asserted the supernatural character of the incident, claiming the voice as a witness to His doctrine. « This voice », He said, « came not because of me but for your sakes », and further on the Evangelist adds that on account of the many manifestations of the Divine power which took place during the last few days of the Master's life on earth among the chief rulers, etc., many believed on him, but, because of the Pharisees, they did not confess him, lest they should be put out of the Synagogue.

The Chief Priests ask Jesus by whose authority He acts.

The Chief Priests ask Jesus by whose authority He acts
Saint Luke — Chap. 20

T factum est in una dierum, docente illo populum in templo et evangelizante convenerunt principes sacerdotum et scribæ cum senioribus,

2. Et aiunt dicentes ad illum : Dic nobis, in qua potestate hæc facis? aut quis est, qui dedit tibi hanc potestatem?

ND it came to pass, *that* on one of those days, as he taught the people in the temple, and preached the gospel, the chief priests and the scribes came upon *him* with the elders,

2. And spake unto him, saying, Tell us, by what authority doest thou these things? or who is he that gave thee this authority?

3. Respondens autem Jesus dixit ad illos : Interrogabo vos et ego unum verbum; respondete mihi :

4. Baptismus Joannis de cœlo erat, an ex hominibus?

5. At illi cogitabant intra se, dicentes: Quia si dixerimus : De cœlo, dicet : Quare ergo non credidistis illi?

6. Si autem dixerimus : Ex hominibus, plebs universa lapidabit nos; certi sunt enim Joannem prophetam esse.

7. Et responderunt se nescire unde esset.

8. Et Jesus ait illis : Neque ego dico vobis in qua potestate hæc facio.

3. And he answered and said unto them, I will also ask you one thing; and answer me :

4. The baptism of John, was it from heaven, or of men?

5. And they reasoned with themselves, saying, If we shall say, From heaven; he will say, Why then believed ye him not?

6. But and if we say, Of men ; all the people will stone us : for they be persuaded that John was a prophet.

7. And they answered, that they could not tell whence *it was*.

8. And Jesus said unto them, Neither tell I you by what authority I do these things.

My picture represents the scene as having taken place about eleven o'clock in the Court of the Gentiles. Many people are seated in the shade in the " Naos Basilica " of Herod. Jesus is going from group to group teaching. In the background behind Him is the western Portico and the Gate leading to the town, corresponding with that now called the " Gate of the Chain ". On the right is the terrace of the Chel, already several times described; in this same building, surrounding the Court of the Women and itself in its turn encircled by the Chel, live the families engaged in the service of the Temple. Amongst others was that of Abtinos, who, as related above, had the secret of preparing the incense used in the Temple.

Esplanade of the Haram

In the same chapter as that just quoted we have a fresh proof of the great influence which had been exercised by John the Baptist, the forerunner of the Lord, and of the extent to which that influence had spread throughout the country. Challenged by Jesus to say in what name John had baptized and to tell Him whether the baptism of John was from Heaven or of men, the great men of the Jews, the Scribes, the Pharisees and the Chief Priests, formidable though their power was over the minds of their fellow-citizens, yet feared that the popular fury might turn upon them and that the people would stone them as blasphemers if they ventured even to throw a doubt on the divine mission of the son of Zacharias. In the words: Plebs universa lapidabit nos, they did indeed express their belief in the unanimity of the whole nation.

The Corner Stone
Saint Matthew — Chap. 21

icit illis Jesus : Numquam legistis in Scripturis : Lapidem quem reprobaverunt ædificantes, hic factus est in caput anguli? A Domino factum est istud, et est mirabile in oculis nostris?

43. Ideo dico vobis, quia auferetur a vobis regnum Dei, et dabitur genti facienti fructus ejus.

44. Et qui ceciderit super lapidem istum, confringetur ; super quem vero ceciderit, conteret eum.

45. Et quum audissent principes sacerdotum et Pharisæi parabolas ejus, cognoverunt, quod de ipsis diceret.

46. Et quærentes eum tenere, timuerunt turbas, quoniam sicut prophetam eum habebant.

esus saith unto them, Did ye never read in the scriptures, The stone which the builders rejected, the same is become the head of the corner : this is the Lord's doing, and it is marvellous in our eyes?

43. Therefore say I unto you, The kingdom of God shall be taken from you, and given to a nation bringing forth the fruits thereof.

44. And whosoever shall fall on this stone shall be broken : but on whomsoever it shall fall, it will grind him to powder.

45. And when the chief priests and Pharisees had heard his parables, they perceived that he spake of them.

46. But when they sought to lay hands on him, they feared the multitude, because they took him for a prophet.

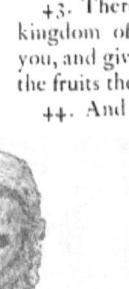

An Armenian

The more important buildings of the Temple were built of Jerusalem limestone of a yellowish white colour. The upper portion of the sanctuary was faced with white marble

veined with blue, which, according to some who saw it, made it look like a mountain of snow, whilst others compared it to the waves of the sea. The supplementary buildings of the Temple surrounding the Court of the Men and the Court of the Women were decorated in another fashion. According to the Talmud, they were faced with red and yellow stones, which had been hewn out of certain quarries near Jerusalem and which are, the red stones at least, peculiar to this one district. The stones, says the Talmud, were arranged in a net-like pattern, that is to say, in squares resembling those of the meshes of a net or, to express it somewhat differently, like a red and yellow chess-board. We can get an idea of the mode of decoration in some of the Mosques still to be seen at Cairo, amongst others that of Sultan Kalaun: in fact, Mahommedan Mosques were often decorated with something of Jewish feeling, so that they often to a certain extent resembled the Temple of Jerusalem. In spite of their beautiful appearance, however, the stone we have just described crumbled away under the action of inclement weather, one or two blocks falling to pieces whilst the rest remained intact. No doubt, a reserve of stones was kept for replacing those thus destroyed, and some corner of one of the courts would be set apart as a work-yard for necessary repairs. There lay the beautiful stone left unused by the builders in the first instance and

The Corner Stone.

on the brink of rejection as an encumbrance, when, after a severe and damp winter, some corner-stone of the Temple in a conspicuous and important portion of the building would become so disintegrated that it had to be taken out, leading to the substitution for it in a place of honour of the beautiful stone originally rejected. This was the idea I have illustrated in my picture, taking it for granted that Jesus, according to His usual custom, took an actual and well-known fact to enforce His doctrine and render it more striking. We may, however, also suppose that Our Lord merely turned to account a proverbial expression several times employed in the Bible, in Psalm cxviii, verse 22, for instance, which is quoted word for word in the Gospel narrative. In favour of the latter interpretation is the fact that Jesus would Himself remember the words of the Old Testament, and it was from the very same Psalm that the Jews took the exclamation with which they hailed the approach of Christ on Palm Sunday : " Blessed is he that cometh in the name of the Lord ".

The Tribute Money
Saint Luke – Chap. 20

t observantes miserunt insidiatores, qui se justos simularent, ut caperent eum in sermone, ut traderent illum principatui et potestati præsidis.

21. Et interrogaverunt eum dicentes: Magister, scimus quia recte dicis et

ND they watched *him*, and sent forth spies, which should feign themselves just men, that they might take hold of his words, that so they might deliver him unto the power and authority of the governor.

21. And they asked him, saying, Master, we know that thou sayest and

doces, et non accipis personam, sed viam Dei in veritate doces :

22. Licet nobis tributum dare Cæsari, an non?

23. Considerans autem dolum illorum dixit ad eos : Quid me tentatis ?

24. Ostendite mihi denarium. Cujus habet imaginem et inscriptionem? Respondentes dixerunt ei : Cæsaris.

25. Et ait illis : Reddite ergo quæ sunt Cæsaris Cæsari, et quæ sunt Dei Deo.

26. Et non potuerunt verbum ejus reprehendere coram plebe, et mirati in responso ejus tacuerunt.

teachest rightly, neither acceptest thou the person *of any*, but teachest the way of God truly :

22. Is it lawful for us to give tribute unto Cæsar, or no?

23. But he perceived their craftiness, and said unto them, Why tempt ye me?

24. Shew me a penny. Whose image and superscription hath it? They answered and said, Cæsar's.

25. And he said unto them, Render therefore unto Cæsar the things which be Cæsar's, and unto God the things which be God's.

26. And they could not take hold of his words before the people : and they marvelled at his answer, and held their peace.

It is morning, and in front of the Jewish notables rise the fifteen steps called the Psalms or the Degrees. On the left of these steps, beneath the green marble columns of the Court of Israel, can be seen the entrance to the rooms where the musicians keep their instruments. In the background, on the south-west, at the corner of the Court of the Women, where we now are, is the room or the pavilion, open to the sky, where the wine and oil were kept. We know that there were three other such pavilions, that of the Nazarites on the south-east, that where the wood to be used in the sacrifices was sorted, on the north-east, and, lastly, that on the north-west, reserved for the use of lepers.

Half-way up the Mount of Olives.

At first sight, the way in which the enemies of Jesus endeavoured to compromise Him seems strange enough. They do not ask if they must pay tribute to Cæsar, which, in case of a reply in the affirmative, might have made Him odious in the eyes of the crowd, who were intensely irritated by the fiscal exactions of the Romans, but they asked " Is it lawful? " a truly singular enquiry when the very real suzerainty of the Roman Emperor over the Jewish people is borne in mind. Never throughout the whole course of the history of the Jews had they refused to pay tribute to the suzerain, whether that suzerain ruled from Nineveh, from Babylon or from Persia. The Pharisees, however, had found means to arouse scruples on this point, and the people would evidently have been ready enough to adopt them. But Jesus, perceiving their craftiness, simply said, to put them to confusion. « Shew me a penny. » The current coin no longer bore the proud device engraved on that in use in the time of the Esmonean or Maccabean princes; Jerusalem the Holy, but simply the effigy of the reigning Emperor Tiberius. The consequence was evident enough, the superscription convincing; they had to pay. For all that, however, the answer of Jesus did not prevent the Pharisees from saying later to Pilate : « he forbids the giving of tribute to Cæsar. »

The Pharisees question Jesus
Saint Mark — Chap. 12

r accessit unus de scribis, qui audierat illos conquirentes, et videns quoniam bene illis responderit, interrogavit eum, quod esset primum omnium mandatum.

29. Jesus autem respondit ei : Quia primum omnium mandatum est : Audi Israel, Dominus Deus tuus Deus unus est,

30. Et diliges Dominum Deum tuum ex toto corde tuo, et ex tota anima tua, et ex tota mente tua, et ex tota virtute tua. Hoc est primum mandatum.

31. Secundum autem simile est illi : Diliges proximum tuum tamquam te ipsum. Majus horum aliud mandatum non est.

ND one of the scribes came, and having heard them reasoning together, and perceiving that he had answered them well, asked him, Which is the first commandment of all ?

29. And Jesus answered him, The first of all the commandments *is*, Hear, O Israel; The Lord our God is one Lord :

30. And thou shalt love the Lord thy God with all thy heart, and with all thy soul, and with all thy mind, and with all thy strength : this *is* the first commandment.

31. And the second *is* like, *namely* this, Thou shalt love thy neighbour as thyself. There is none other commandment greater than these.

Saint Luke.

HOLY WEEK

The Pharisees question Jesus.

32. Et ait illi scriba : Bene, Magister; in veritate dixisti, quia unus est Deus, et non est alius præter eum;

33. Et ut diligatur ex toto corde, et ex toto intellectu, et ex tota anima, et ex tota fortitudine, et diligere proximum tamquam se ipsum, majus est omnibus holocautomatibus et sacrificiis.

34. Jesus autem videns, quod sapienter respondisset, dixit illi: Non es longe a regno Dei. Et nemo jam audebat eum interrogare.

32. And the scribe said unto him, Well, Master, thou hast said the truth : for there is none other but he :

33. And to love him with all the heart, and with all the understanding, and with all the soul, and with all the strength, and to love *his* neighbour as himself, is more than all whole burnt offerings and sacrifices.

34. And when Jesus saw that he answered discreetly, he said unto him, Thou art not far from the kingdom of God. And no man after that durst ask him *any question*.

« Woe unto you, Scribes and Pharisees ! »

Woe unto you, Scribes and Pharisees
Saint Matthew — Chap. 23

 UNC Jesus locutus est ad turbas et ad discipulos suos,
2. Dicens : Super cathedram Moysi sederunt scribæ et Pharisæi.
3. Omnia ergo quæcumque dixerint vobis servate et facite, secundum opera vero eorum nolite facere : dicunt enim, et non faciunt.
4. Alligant enim onera gravia et im-

 HEN spake Jesus to the multitude, and to his disciples,
2. Saying, The scribes and the Pharisees sit in Moses' seat :
3. All therefore whatsoever they bid you observe, *that* observe and do; but do not ye after their works : for they say, and do not.
4. For they bind heavy burdens and

portabilia, et imponunt in humeros hominum, digito autem suo nolunt ea movere.

5. Omnia vero opera sua faciunt ut videantur ab hominibus; dilatant enim phylacteria sua et magnificant fimbrias.

6. Amant autem primos recubitus in cœnis et primas cathedras in synagogis,

7. Et salutationes in foro, et vocari ab hominibus Rabbi.

8. Vos autem nolite vocari Rabbi; unus est enim Magister vester, omnes autem vos fratres estis.

9. Et patrem nolite vocare vobis super terram: unus est enim Pater vester, qui in cœlis est.

10. Nec vocemini magistri, quia Magister vester unus est, Christus.

11. Qui major est vestrum, erit minister vester.

12. Qui autem se exaltaverit humiliabitur, et qui se humiliaverit exaltabitur.

13. Væ autem vobis, scribæ et Pharisæi hypocritæ, quia clauditis regnum cœlorum ante homines; vos enim non intratis, nec introeuntes sinitis intrare.

grievous to be borne, and lay *them* on men's shoulders; but they *themselves* will not move them with one of their fingers.

5. But all their works they do for to be seen of men: they make broad their phylacteries, and enlarge the borders of their garments,[2]

6. And love the uppermost rooms at feasts, and the chief seats in the synagogues,

7. And greetings in the markets, and to be called of men, Rabbi, Rabbi.

8. But be not ye called Rabbi: for one is your Master, *even* Christ; and all ye are brethren.

9. And call no *man* your father upon the earth: for one is your Father, which is in heaven.

10. Neither be ye called masters: for one is your Master, *even* Christ.

11. But he that is greatest among you shall be your servant.

12. And whosoever shall exalt himself shall be abased; and he that shall humble himself shall be exalted.

13. But woe unto you, scribes and Pharisees, hypocrites! for ye shut up the kingdom of heaven against men: for ye neither go in *yourselves*, neither suffer ye them that are entering to go in.

One of the Silome.

14. Væ vobis, scribæ et Pharisæi hypocritæ, quia comeditis domos viduarum, orationes longas orantes; propter hoc amplius accipietis judicium.

15. Væ vobis, scribæ et Pharisæi hypocritæ, quia circuitis mare et aridam, ut faciatis unum proselytum; et quum fuerit factus, facitis eum filium gehennæ duplo quam vos.

16. Væ vobis, duces cæci, qui dicitis : Quicumque juraverit per templum, nihil est; qui autem juraverit in auro templi, debet.

33. Serpentes, genimina viperarum, quomodo fugietis a judicio gehennæ ?

14. Woe unto you, scribes and Pharisees, hypocrites! for ye devour widows' houses, and for a pretence make long prayers : therefore ye shall receive the greater damnation.

15. Woe unto you, scribes and Pharisees, hypocrites! for ye compass sea and land to make one proselyte, and when he is made, ye make him twofold more the child of hell than yourselves.

16. Woe unto you, ye blind guides, which say, Whosoever shall swear by the temple, it is nothing ; but whosoever shall swear by the gold of the temple, he is a debtor!

33. Ye serpents, ye generation of vipers, how can ye escape the damnation of hell?

A typical Jew.

The Court of the Gentiles where Jesus was, was paved with polished stones which had been restored by Herod. It was washed, indeed flooded with water every morning, and to strangers visiting it for the first time it looked like a lake, so vividly did the polished floor reflect the surrounding buildings. A similar effect may be noticed in the vast court of the Mehemet-Ali Mosque at Cairo, where the alabaster pavement, especially in the morning, looks like a great pool just about to overflow its banks.

Jerusalem, Jerusalem!
Saint Matthew — Chap. 23

ERUSALEM, Jerusalem, quæ occidis prophetas, et lapidas eos qui ad te missi sunt, quoties volui congregare

Jerusalem, Jerusalem, *thou* that killest the prophets, and stonest them which are sent unto thee, how often

filios tuos, quemadmodum gallina congregat pullos suos sub alas, et noluisti.

38. Ecce relinquetur vobis domus vestra deserta.

39. Dico enim vobis, non me videbitis amodo, donec dicatis: Benedictus, qui venit in nomine Domini.

would I have gathered thy children together, even as a hen gathereth her chickens under *her* wings, and ye would not!

38. Behold, your house is left unto you desolate.

39. For I say unto you, Ye shall not see me henceforth, till ye shall say, Blessed *is* he that cometh in the name of the Lord.

Standing in Solomon's Porch, where He ever loved to be, Jesus has the town beneath Him, and Mount Zion, just now wrapped in shadow, rising above the western porch. On the right can be seen the southern side of the Temple buildings surrounded by the rampart of the Chel. There is the Water-gate, or the south-eastern entrance to the Court of the Women. The day is now drawing to a close; the shadows of the buildings and porticoes are lengthening, indicating that it is about the ninth hour, or three o'clock in the afternoon. Soon the sun, still bathing the town with its light, will sink behind her and leave her in twilight. Jesus foresees that the city will ere long in her turn desert Him, and He mourns over the approaching fate of the ungrateful town. He is not the first she has rejected; she had treated the prophets and the messengers from on high in a similar manner, as if she had made up her mind to remain blind. Jesus mourns over this obstinate blindness and grieves at the thought of the punishment it will bring.

The Widow's mite.

The Widow's mite
Saint Mark – Chap. 12

T sedens Jesus contra gazophylacium, adspiciebat quomodo turba jactaret æs in gazophylacium, et multi divites jactabant multa.

ND Jesus sat over against the treasury, and beheld how the people cast money into the treasury : and many that were rich cast in much.

42. Quum venisset autem vidua una pauper, misit duo minuta, quod est quadrans.

43. Et convocans discipulos suos ait illis: Amen dico vobis, quoniam vidua hæc pauper plus omnibus misit, qui miserunt in gazophylacium.

44. Omnes enim ex eo, quod abundabat illis, miserunt, hæc vero de penuria sua omnia, quæ habuit misit, totum victum suum.

42. And there came a certain poor widow, and she threw in two mites, which make a farthing.

43. And he called *unto him* his disciples, and saith unto them, Verily I say unto you, That this poor widow hath cast more in, than all they which have cast into the treasury:

44. For all *they* did cast in of their abundance; but she of her want did cast in all that she had, *even* all her living.

A disciple from the South.

The Greek name for the Court of the Women is Gazophylacium, or the Court of the Treasure, given to it on account of the thirteen chests placed at each of the five entrances, in which were deposited the various offerings brought to the Temple. These chests were of a curious and peculiar shape, and were made up of a collection of copper tubes of a greater or lesser length, according to the position they occupied in the general receptacle in which they were grouped. At the orifice of each tube was an inscription stating what kind of offerings were to be placed in it, and the pieces of money dropped into the openings went down the tube reserved for them into the interior of the chest, whence they were afterwards removed by the Priests. To prevent the clever contrivances by means of which thieves used to get at the money by introducing a stick or a line smeared with pitch, under pretence of putting their own offerings in, the tubes were made of a conical shape, broadening downwards from the narrow opening. Thanks to this peculiarity, these collections of copper conduits looked very much like a group of trumpets, hence the popular name given to them. Outside the entrance to the Gazophylacium was a kind of vestibule provided with seats against the walls affording a good position for watching the passers-by and noting the behaviour of those who brought offerings. On this occasion Jesus too was seated there, resting after an exhausting day of teaching. He saw the various groups of pilgrims pass by who had come up to the Temple for the festivals and had brought with them their voluntary offerings, and amongst them were many wealthy men who ostentatiously dropped in their generous gifts, whilst a widow also came in her turn and threw in two mites « all her living ». Saint Mark explains to his Roman readers that the Greek word used meant half a quadrans: now the Roman quadrans was the fourth part of an as and the as was equal to rather less than an English farthing, so that the widow's two mites were scarcely as much as that. But for all that they represented "all her living", and this was why Jesus commended her so highly, and anxious that the example should not be lost on His disciples, He called them together and praised the poor woman in their hearing, saying she "hath cast more in than all they which have cast into the Treasury". It was this touching and pathetic episode that ended a day which had been full of eager disputation. Just before Jesus had been reproaching the Pharisees with devouring widows' houses and for a pretence making long prayers: He now calls our attention to one of the poor widows ruined by the pretended worshippers of God, consecrating to the service of the Lord all that they had left to her.

Steps in the Haram.

The Disciples
ADMIRE THE BUILDINGS OF THE TEMPLE
Saint Mark – Chap. 13

 T quum egrederetur de templo, ait illi unus ex discipulis suis: Magister, adspice quales lapides et quales structuræ.

2. Et respondens Jesus ait illi: Vides has omnes magnas ædificationes? Non relinquetur lapis super lapidem, qui non destruatur.

 ND as he went out of the temple, one of his disciples saith unto him, Master, see what manner of stones and what buildings *are here!*

2. And Jesus answering said unto him, Seest thou these great buildings? there shall not be left one stone upon another, that shall not be thrown down.

The group of Jesus and His disciples are leaving the Temple by the new gateway built by Herod the Great. It was the one which led to the Valley of Jehoshaphat and to Bethany.

The Disciples admire the Buildings of the Temple.

whither Jesus was bound. It was low down in comparison with the platform of the Court of the Gentiles, to which a flight of steps led up, and it opened on to a mass of houses occupied by the work-people employed at the Temple. It was from this gateway that the High Priest and his assistants issued on their way to the Mount of Olives to burn the red heifer. In my picture can be seen the northern side of the Temple buildings and the Chel, where can also be made out a pavilion or watch-tower occupied by Levites, this part of the Temple being but little frequented. On the right a glimpse is obtained of the northern portico, adjoining which are the outbuildings of the Antonia Citadel. It shows the background beyond the watch-tower of the Levites, and, outflanking the Temple itself, for it is outside the sacred precincts, is the building known as El-Moked, already described. Quite on the right can be seen the entrance to the buildings set apart for the attendants in charge of the animals for sacrifice, who from it could easily reach the Sheep-pool.

There was a striking peculiarity about the departure of Jesus from the Temple on this occasion, for He was leaving it never to return. It was the evening of Holy Tuesday, and on the Wednesday His death was to be decided on. Hence the terrible prophecy uttered by Him which contrasts so ominously with the naive admiration of His disciples and assumes the character of a malediction. " See what manner of stones and what buildings are here! " said the twelve. And truly from this point of view the Temple walls did present a most imposing appearance, for Josephus asserts that most of the blocks which had been used in their construction measured twenty-five cubits in length by twelve in width and eight in height.

The Prophecy of the destruction of the Temple.

The Prophecy of the destruction of the Temple
Saint Mark — Chap. 13

T quum sederet in monte Olivarum contra templum, interrogabant eum separatim Petrus et Jacobus et Joannes et Andreas :

4. Dic nobis, quando ista fient? et quod signum erit, quando hæc omnia incipient consummari?

5. Et respondens Jesus cœpit dicere

ND as he sat upon the mount of Olives over against the temple, Peter and James and John and Andrew asked him privately,

4. Tell us, when shall these things be? and what *shall be* the sign when all these things shall be fulfilled?

5. And Jesus answering them began to

illis : Videte, ne quis vos seducat ;

6. Multi enim venient in nomine meo dicentes : Quia ego sum, et multos seducent.

7. Quum audieritis autem bella et opiniones bellorum, ne timueritis; oportet enim hæc fieri, sed nondum finis.

8. Exsurget enim gens contra gentem et regnum super regnum, et erunt terræ motus per loca, et fames. Initium dolorum hæc.

9. Videte autem vosmetipsos. Tradent enim vos in conciliis, et in synagogis vapulabitis, et ante præsides et reges stabitis propter me in testimonium illis.

10. Et in omnes gentes primum oportet prædicari evangelium.

11. Et quum duxerint vos tradentes, nolite præcogitare quid loquamini, sed quod datum vobis fuerit in illa hora, id loquimini; non enim vos estis loquentes, sed Spiritus sanctus.

12. Tradet autem frater fratrem in mortem et pater filium, et consurgent

say, Take heed lest any *man* deceive you :

6. For many shall come in my name, saying, I am *Christ*; and shall deceive many.

7. And when ye shall hear of wars and rumours of wars, be ye not troubled : for *such things* must needs be ; but the end *shall* not *be* yet.

8. For nation shall rise against nation, and kingdom against kingdom : and there shall be earthquakes in divers places, and there shall be famines and troubles : these *are* the beginnings of sorrows.

9. But take heed to yourselves : for they shall deliver you up to councils ; and in the synagogues ye shall be beaten : and ye shall be brought before rulers and kings for my sake, for a testimony against them.

10. And the gospel must first be published among all nations.

11. But when they shall lead *you*, and deliver you up, take no thought beforehand what ye shall speak, neither do ye premeditate : but whatsoever shall be given you in that hour, that speak ye : for it is not ye that speak, but the Holy Ghost.

12. Now the brother shall betray the brother to death, and the father the son;

A corner of the Haram, on the supposed site of the Temple.

filii in parentes et morte afficient eos.

13. Et eritis odio omnibus propter nomen meum. Qui autem sustinuerit in finem, hic salvus erit.

14. Quum autem videritis abominationem desolationis, stantem ubi non debet (qui legit intelligat), tunc qui in Judæa sunt fugiant in montes.

and children shall rise up against *their* parents, and shall cause them to be put to death.

13. And ye shall be hated of all *men* for my name's sake ; but he that shall endure unto the end, the same shall be saved.

14. But when ye shall see the abomination of desolation, spoken of by Daniel the prophet, standing where it ought not (let him that readeth understand), then let them that be in Judæa flee to the mountains.

An Armenian.

In the Valley of Jehoshaphat, half-way up the Mount of Olives, there were several resting-places for the use of the Priests of the Temple, planted with such trees as the terebinth or turpentine, the locust, mulberry and cypress. When the wars came these resting-places were, of course, deserted and neglected, rapidly reverting to waste lands. They were, however, still the property of the Jews, though they were appropriated first by the Christians and later by the Mussulmans. They are now spoken of as belonging to the Mosques, that is to say, they are looked upon as municipal districts under the control of the religious authorities, embankments and excavations indicating very clearly the use to which they are put. Here it was that Jesus and the few Apostles admitted to close intimacy with Him went and sat down over against the Temple contra templum *after leaving it for the last time. Then, in full view of the imposing mass of the celebrated buildings, which looked as if they were destined to last for ever, Jesus solemnly prophesied their destruction.*

Mary Magdalene's box of very precious ointment
Saint Matthew — Chap. 26

um autem Jesus esset in Bethania, in domo Simonis leprosi,

7. Accessit ad eum mulier habens alabastrum unguenti pretiosi, et effudit super caput ipsius recumbentis.

ow when Jesus was in Bethany, in the house of Simon the leper,

7. There came unto him a woman having an alabaster box of very precious ointment, and poured it on his head, as he sat *at meat*.

8. Videntes autem discipuli indignati sunt, dicentes : Ut quid perditio hæc?

9. Potuit enim istud venundari multo, et dari pauperibus.

10. Sciens autem Jesus ait illis : Quid molesti estis huic mulieri? opus enim bonum operata est in me.

11. Nam semper pauperes habetis vobiscum, me autem non semper habetis.

12. Mittens enim hæc unguentum

8. But when his disciples saw *it*, they had indignation, saying, To what purpose *is* this waste?

9. For this ointment might have been sold for much, and given to the poor.

10. When Jesus understood *it*, he said unto them, Why trouble ye the woman? for she hath wrought a good work upon me.

11. For ye have the poor always with you; but me ye have not always.

12. For in that she hath poured this

hoc in corpus meum, ad sepeliendum me fecit.

13. Amen dico vobis, ubicumque prædicatum fuerit hoc evangelium in toto mundo, dicetur et quod hæc fecit in memoriam ejus.

ointment on my body, she did *it* for my burial.

13. Verily I say unto you, Wheresoever this gospel shall be preached in the whole world, *there* shall also this, that this woman hath done, be told for a memorial of her.

The Jews conspire together.

In connection with our account of the marriage at Cana we have already described how the rooms used at festivals were arranged in Palestine. The low table was generally of a horse-shoe shape, and the guests reclined on the outer side of the circle, leaning on the left arm, so as to have the right arm free. The women did not eat with the men, but generally remained in an adjoining room or in a kind of extension of the arcades of the dining hall itself, separated from the men by a trellis-work partition. They could thus see all that was going on and if necessary give an opportune word of advice, as Mary the mother of Jesus did at Cana.

With a room thus arranged, and bearing in mind the ready hospitality of Oriental houses, Mary Magdalene could quite easily slip in unperceived behind the guests. Draped in her garments of penitence, which attracted no attention, she was able to pass like a shadow behind Jesus, break open the flask of perfumed ointment she had brought with her, which was no bigger than a fig, and pour a little of its contents on the head of her Master. Then, kneeling down, she spread the rest over His sacred feet, which she was able to reach without difficulty as they rested on the couch. Her anointing finished, she proceeded to wipe away the surplus ointment with her long hair, and the house was filled with the penetrating and medicinal odour of the spikenard, which was then much used in religious worship and at funerals. Her act of pious homage duly performed, Mary Magdalene was for stealing quietly away, but the scent of the ointment betrayed her and gave rise to the disparaging remarks and murmurs against her of the guests, especially of Judas. This incident, in fact, seems to have given the final blow to the wavering fidelity of that disciple. He began boasting, talking about the necessity of economy and pretending to take a great interest in the poor, really, as Saint John points out, only betraying his own avarice and dishonesty, which were already notorious. Jesus, having rebuked him before everyone by His high commendation of what Mary Magdalene had done, the unfortunate Judas, wounded to the quick and already a traitor at heart, rose from the table and went out to put his evil design into execution.

Transept of the El-Aksa Mosque.

WEDNESDAY

The Jews conspire together
Saint Mark — Chap. 14

ERAT autem Pascha et azyma post biduum, et quærebant summi sacerdotes et scribæ, quomodo eum dolo tenerent et occiderent.

FTER two days was *the feast of* the passover, and of unleavened bread : and the chief priests and the scribes sought how they might take him by craft, and put *him* to death.

The death of Jesus had long been decided on; indeed, ever since His miracles had grown so striking and His popularity had appeared to become a menace to the authority of the Chief Priests, the latter had determined to destroy Him. The question now was not, therefore, as to His fate but as to the best means of securing His person without causing a tumult amongst the people. Once in their hands He could not escape, for, in the case of a judicial sentence being found impossible, these men would not have hesitated to assassinate Him privately. In any case, however, they judged it prudent to put off the execution of Jesus until after the celebration of the feast, for fear of trouble with the assembled crowds. Under certain circumstances, the carrying out of legal sentences was put off until the concourse of pilgrims should add to the solemnity, but in this case the very sacredness of the time would have constituted a danger, more especially as the chief partizans of Jesus were amongst the turbulent and sturdy Galileans, ever ready for a conflict, and it was no rare thing in Judæa for riots to take place during the great festivals. The postponement of the execution was therefore voted, but it was at the same time determined to watch for a favorable opportunity for an early arrest. After all, these resolutions came to naught, because Jesus was put to death just at the most solemn moment of the feast and therefore, with the greatest possible éclat. The Sanhedrin, in fact,

Exhortation to the Sinner.

doubtless perceived that the popularity of Jesus had not such deep root as they had thought, and the defection of one of the twelve confirmed them in this opinion. They therefore reverted to their original idea and determination to give to their victory all the noisy celebrity for which their hatred craved.

Judas goes to the Chief Priests.

Judas goes to the Chief Priests
Saint Mark — Chap. 14

T Judas Iscariotes, unus de duodecim, abiit ad summos sacerdotes, ut proderet eum illis.

11. Qui audientes gavisi sunt, et promiserunt ei pecuniam se daturos. Et quærebat quomodo illum opportune traderet.

ND Judas Iscariot, one of the twelve, went unto the chief priests, to betray him unto them.

11. And when they heard *it*, they were glad, and promised to give him money. And he sought how he might conveniently betray him.

Christ going to the Mount of Olives at night.

Christ going to the Mount of Olives at night
Saint Luke -- Chap. 21, v. 37

RAT autem diebus docens in templo, noctibus vero exiens morabatur in monte, qui vocatur Oliveti.

ND in the day time he was teaching in the temple; and at night he went out, and abode in the mount that is called *the mount* of Olives.

HOLY WEEK

We have seen that when Jesus was in Galilee He often retired at night to some lofty place to pray; when He was in Judæa He continued to do the same, and the Evangelists speak of the Mount of Olives as His retreat when night fell. This choice of special localities remarkable for their height and isolation is a striking peculiarity in the life of Our Lord, but it was also a traditional Jewish custom to pray in elevated spots, because height was alike symbolic and provocative of the aspirations of the Spirit. Jesus, Whose life was one long prayer, and Who needed no stimulus to lead Him to long after God with His whole soul, was yet willing to comply with what were to a certain extent the requirements of ritual, and to encompass about His solemn devotions with the solemnity of the mountains and of the night. May we not suppose, in spite of the silence of the Evangelist, that in these days so near the death of the Master, the Mount of Olives was not the only height which witnessed His petitions? Near to it there was a spot from which also He could behold the beloved city and which must have attracted Him more than any other, for that spot was Golgotha, where He was so soon to complete His work. May not Jesus have gone there secretly to pray and to commune with His Father in some mysterious way? May not His soul have been wrapt in an intensely profound meditation, offering up to God in anticipation the approaching sacrifice and mentally rehearsing, as in a realistic vision, the coming scene, so fraught alike with gloom and consolation? We really seem to be justified in imagining something of the kind, for Jesus, in that He was the Son of God as well as the Son of man, could see into the future: now the future for Him, the future of to-morrow was the cross, the cross and Calvary! How could His soul escape a vision, recurring perhaps some twenty times, of the rising up of that cross? How could His feet help being drawn in the direction where it was so soon to be set up?

One of the Messengers of Saint John.

Antique frieze at Jifna on the road from Naplousium to Jerusalem.

THE CLOSE
OF

HOLY WEEK

THE PASSION

THE PASSION

INTRODUCTION

HE hour of the Passion is the supreme hour for Jesus: it is for this hour that He came, as He Himself declares in Saint John, XII. verse 27; He speaks of it constantly; He looks eagerly forward to it, for its arrival is to be the signal for the salvation of mankind. This being so, it will be readily understood that this last portion of my work has been more absorbing than every other, that I have brought to bear on it a yet more minute care in the arrangement of subjects and in the exact interpretation of the facts they recall. Every detail has now an immense value, for it is a portion of the price paid for the redemption of the human race: I have felt, therefore, that not one such detail supplied to us by the Gospel narrative should be omitted, nay, not even one which that narrative justifies us in imagining for ourselves. This is why I have paused at certain subjects which are rarely, if ever, treated, such as *Jesus in Prison*, *The Five Wedges*, *The Scourging of the Face* and *The Scourging of the Back*, *The first Nail*, *What Our Saviour saw from the Cross*, etc. The better to mark the succession of events, to emphasize as much as possible their importance, and at the same time to enable the reader to follow their course with greater ease, I have indicated the chief hours of the sacred drama on a dial which I have several times repeated. Those hours, the passing of which the heavenly hosts must have watched as the most precious and most pregnant with meaning for all time, appeared to me well to deserve to be thus emphasized, and I felt the necessity of gradually, religiously unfolding to the gaze of the spectator each one of the phases of an event the most solemn in the whole history of the world. I said to myself, moreover, that if the Hour of the Passion was indeed the Hour of Jesus, it would be expedient to reserve for that moment the actual and, so to speak, synthetic representation of His person, such at least as my imagination as a painter and my faith as a Christian should enable me to evolve. Hence the three portraits of Our Saviour Jesus Christ: the principal one representing Him as absolutely quiescent, the other two: *Jesus in Prison* and *Jesus leaving the Prætorium*, shewing Him as the Mediator for and the Victim of men. A few night scenes upon which

INTRODUCTION

I naturally came, as it were by the way, were of very special value to me, in that they enabled me to bring out not only more picturesquely but with a more vivid truthfulness that sense of oppression which was so eminently characteristic of all the machinations of the Jews against the Saviour.

One objection has been made to this last portion of my work to which I should like to reply: « Too much blood, too many horrors, too many painful and revolting details introduced with a view to producing a heart-rending effect. » May I be permitted to

Valley of Jehoshaphat, looking towards Shiloh.

remark that those who speak in this way have not understood me. I have already stated what has been my point of view throughout my task: it has been that of an historian, a faithful and conscientious historian. Do people want me to compose an account of the Passion in the style of the poets of the Renaissance? Do they want a well-made crucified figure with a very white skin and three drops of blood at each wound to contrast with the pallor of the flesh? Such a crucified form is not mine, for it is not that of history. Those who are afraid of blood and of wounds, of flesh which turns blue when it is bruised, had better not look at my work and they had better not read the Gospel either. Let me be forgiven for thus bracketing the two together, for each is a work of truth, not of poetic fancy. I attack no one else's theory, I bring no action against any brother artist; every one has his own way of interpreting the same thing, and I can well understand that a point of view very different from my own may be perfectly legitimate; I will even admit, if you like, that it may be absolutely superior, just as an epic poem is, in a certain way, superior to history, but nevertheless history has its value and its rights, indefeasible rights, against which no false delicacy can avail anything.

I suspect, moreover, that the criticism I have first quoted is bound up with another already passed upon me: « There is not », they say, « enough of the ideal in his pictures. » But we have got to come to an understanding as to what is meant by the ideal. What is the exact interpretation of that word, which is made to signify so many things? As for me, the ideal is the truth; I understand truth in the sense in which Plato understood beauty, for, according to that philosopher, beauty and goodness are one. The ideal is truth in its completeness: truth of facts, truth in the interpretation of facts and of their higher meaning. Why should I sacrifice the first of these truths to the second? Are they not compatible? Will they not be useful to each other? When Leonardo painted the Last Supper at Santa-

Maria-Grazie at Milan, he doubtless painted the truth; but only moral truth as interpreted by him, not actual historic truth. When, on the other hand, some realist or so-called realist, some archæologist-painter such as is now to be often met with, represents the Last Supper of Jesus exactly as he would that of some Jew contemporary with Our Lord, he may give us more or less historic truth, but he misses moral truth altogether. As for me, I have tried as far as possible to combine the two. I wished my Christ to be a true Christ, that is to say, a God-Man as truly Man as He is God, and, again, not a mere ordinary man, but just the Man and no other revealed in the Gospel to every one who reads it with an unprejudiced mind. In thus treating my subject, in so far at least as I have succeeded in my endeavour, I could not miss the ideal, for the true Christ is the realization of the ideal; what good would it have been, then, to distort facts with a view to giving them a kind of factitious ideality very inferior to that which is already innate in them? According to my idea, it was far better to confine myself strictly to the truth as far as that truth is accessible, and this is the kind of ideal which it has ever been my aim to attain. Whether I have or have not attained it, it is not for me to determine. I make but one claim: that my intention was good, and, if the result is not approved of, the blame must be laid on my hand alone.

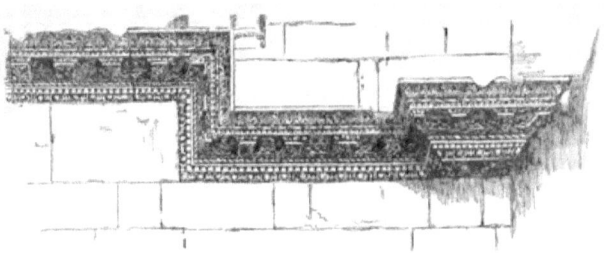

Antique cornice let into the wall of the Church of the Holy Sepulchre at Jerusalem.

Capital from the El-Aksa Mosque.

North-east angle of Jerusalem.

Jerusalem

THE view here given is a restoration of Jerusalem as seen from the Mount of Olives, near Mount Scopus, where Titus encamped his troops during the siege, and where the Galileans also camped when they came up to Jerusalem for the Feast of Pentecost. The whole town was, in fact, surrounded by the camps of the different Jewish tribes who came up for the various ceremonies, which explains the reference of Josephus to the millions of inhabitants during the time of Pentecost, and is proved by the immense number of victims offered up in sacrifice. King Agrippa, wishing to know exactly how many people came to Jerusalem for the festivals, said to the Priests: « Set aside one kidney for me from each lamb sacrificed. » The Rabbis set aside six hundred thousand kidneys, which, as each lamb offered represented ten persons, gives a total of six million Jews. On the left could be seen the pigeons, numbers of which, it is said, used to perch on two cedars near the bridge over the brook Kedron. Under one of these trees there were four shops in which various wares considered legally pure were sold. One shop alone disposed of forty sacks of pigeons a month, which would be enough to supply all the offerings of the kind for the whole of the Jewish people. The gate seen in my picture is that known as the Sheep-gate. In the town near this gate is the Sheep-pool, where the sheep for sacrifice were washed. Farther away is the massive Antonia Tower and its out-buildings, whilst at the highest point of the town is the Palace of Herod with the Hippicus, Mariamne and Phasaleus Towers. Near the Palace, the walls of which form a retreat, can be seen Golgotha and the Holy Sepulchre, which about ten years after the death of Herod became included in the town by the building of the new wall begun by Herod Agrippa, which he was unable to complete, as he died soon afterwards in Cæsarea. The town is shewn cut across by

THE PASSION

rows of walls flanked by towers; these are the various enceintes added from time to time, with

Walls of Jerusalem on the northern side.

a view to the enlargement of the City. Beyond the last of the walls on the left can be seen the Valley of Hinnom where the Apostles took refuge on Holy Thursday, after their Master had been arrested. Above the valley rises the Hill of Evil Counsel, where Caiaphas decided to put Jesus to death.

The Temple challenges attention on account of its vast size. The smoke ascending to Heaven from it rises from the Altar of Burnt Sacrifice, and is produced by the burning of the wood, flesh and fat which are being consumed on that altar. Quite close to it is the Oulem or vestibule of the Temple properly so called; the entrance is hidden by the thick Babylonian curtain which, however, only extends half-way up the opening, so as to allow of the escape of the clouds of smoke from the incense offered up in the Hekal or Holy Place. The Court of the Women can be made out in front of a little dome which separates it from the Court of the Men and from that of the Priests. It was on this dome that Pilate set up the Roman eagles, causing a rebellion, for the young men of the town dragged them down with ropes. The buildings surrounding this court were set apart for various purposes which have already been partly described: on the left of the Nicanor Gate lived the family of Ablinos, who were possessed of the secret of making incense; in another, salt was kept, yet another was a lavatory. On one side the skins of the victims were salted, on the other their entrails were washed; there was also a small room in which wood was stored. In the room called that of the hewn stones, because it was built entirely of hewn stones, sat the Supreme Council, and beyond it stretched the vast Court of the Gentiles surrounding the various buildings. Then, farther to the left, can be seen the Naos Basilica or Royal Porch, built by Herod, with five naves upheld by Corinthian columns, each one twenty-five cubits or rather more than thirty-six feet high. Jerusalem was built on the highest part of the chain of mountains which divides Judæa, and the Temple being on the loftiest point of the town, the view from it must have extended as far as the Dead Sea. When the west wind blew from the Mediterranean one could hear, at least so say the Rabbis, no less than six different sounds at Jericho, which was six leagues by road and four leagues as the crow flies from Jerusalem. These sounds were: 1. the noise made by the opening of the Temple gates which required eighteen Levites to move them; 2. the music of the organ or Magrepha; 3. the blows which resounded from the pedestal of the basin of bronze; 4. the voice of the Priest summoning the people to the morning service; 5. the music of the flutes and the clashing of the cymbals; and sixth, and last, the voice of the High Priest on the great Day of Atonement, when he pronounced the sacred Tetragrammaton, or great and terrible name of Jehovah. Moreover, the scent of the incense burnt in the Temple also reached Jericho. Thanks to the great height of the site of the Temple, the town itself was lit up at night by the candles in the golden candlesticks in the Court of the Gentiles, the wicks for which were made of the cast-off vestments and sashes of the Priests. When these wicks were of linen the flame rose straight up, but this was not the case if they were of cotton. It is said that on clear nights the women of Jerusalem were able to sort out their wheat by the light of the logs of wood burning on the Altar. In fact, a big fire was made up at night, so that smouldering embers might be found in the morning. In the background of my picture on the right can be seen the mountains at the base of which is the village of Ain-Karim, where Saint Elizabeth dwelt, and near to it is the desert of Saint John the Baptist. On the left is the road leading to Bethlehem, and Hebron is situated behind the loftiest mountain.

On page 75 will be found a second restoration of Jerusalem taken from the south-east. It represents the massive Temple buildings, the actual walls of which have been discovered, as they rose above the Valley of Jehoshaphat. On the left is the suburb of Ophel, succeeded by the upper portion of the town called Sion. Above, at the south-west angle of the walls, can be seen a bridge of three arches, part of the foundations of which still remain in the western wall of the Temple. Built up against the eastern wall is a crowded mass of houses protected by a wall of which some remains have been found in excavations and to which the name of the wall of Nehemiah has been given. These houses originally formed a hamlet in which lived the masons employed in the Temple works : Joseph of Arimathæa was, it is said, the owner of these houses. The débris of the Temple after its destruction and the rubbish flung upon the ruins by order of the Romans, to prevent the Jews from resorting thither to pray, and which went on accumulating for some two or three centuries, was cleared away in obedience to

Omar and thrown over the walls into the Kedron valley, which they completely choked up, at the same time burying the village. Omar himself set the example by throwing the first basketful of rubbish over the wall. All that can now be seen is the top of this enclosure wall, but it was originally something like eighty feet high, as proved by the

South-west angle of the Haram on the site of the Temple, taken from the Gate of the Mugarabees.

measurements taken by English explorers. The viaduct spanning the valley was the road by which the red heifer was led to the Mount of Olives to be sacrificed, and along it the scape-goat also was taken to the desert, a low wall in the centre of the viaduct keeping it apart from the

Modern Jerusalem.

crowd. There was a little bridge over the Kedron built and kept in order at the expense of the High Priest. Each new High Priest, disdaining to use the old bridge, had it thrown down and a new one built at his own cost. More even than that, Simon the Just, having to sacrifice two red heifers during his term of office, would not let the second pass over the bridge which had served for the first, but considered it necessary to have a new bridge built, so that the victim might cross by way of a perfectly untrodden track. It was necessary, moreover, to have a passage in the middle of the bridge reserved for the red heifer and still more for the scape-goat, to protect them from the attacks of the Babylonians, who would come and pull the beard of the goat or otherwise torment it to make it go on faster, crying: " Get along with you! be off and take our sins away! " The bridge was of wood painted red, the colour red being with the Jews emblematical of sin. The scape-goat wore tassels of scarlet wool, which had been fastened on to his forehead by the High Priest, with scarlet bands, and the heifer chosen for sacrifice was also always red, as a symbol of the sin she was to expiate. It will be noticed that the walls immediately surrounding the Sanctuary on the side of the Eastern or Nicanor Gateway are lower than the others; this was to allow the Temple buildings to stand out more distinctly, so that when the High Priest had sacrificed the red heifer he could sprinkle the blood towards the Holy of Holies, for he could see the entrance to it across the Valley of Jehoshaphat. Thanks to this lowness of the walls the exact spot where the entrance to the Sanctuary once stood can be identified near the centre of the rock on which the Mosque of Omar is built; it is also easy to make out where the High

The Heathen Temple in Golgotha.

Priest stood on the Mount of Olives during the offering up of the sacrifice just alluded to. Above the Sanctuary can be seen a flight of crows, a detail founded on the fact of the existence having been proved of a reservoir of water on the flat roof, provided to attract the birds and prevent them from going elsewhere and soiling the other portions of the sacred buildings. Moreover, the Holy of Holies was protected by a roof covered over with gold, and even the vestibule which dominated the pinnacle was covered with plates of gold, whilst the roofs were all set with spikes to keep birds from settling on them. In the background of my picture can be seen the four towers of the Antonia Citadel built by Herod.

After the siege and destruction of Jerusalem the early Christians, who had at first taken refuge at Pella on the other side of the Jordan, returned to Jerusalem. They flocked in crowds to do homage to the spots sanctified by the preaching and the miracles of Jesus. Gradually their numbers increased so much that two hundred years later the Emperor thought their presence worthy of his notice, and, with a view to driving them away, he was not content merely, as already described, to have all the refuse of the town piled up on the site of the Temple, but he also had a temple which he dedicated to Venus erected on the plateau of Golgotha. At the same time he built a temple to Jupiter on the Mount of Olives, from which Jesus had ascended to Heaven, whilst at Bethlehem, on the site of the Caves of the Nativity, he set up yet another temple, dedicated to Adonis. These various desecrations brought about an unexpected result, no doubt through the special intervention of Providence, for it was by this means that the sites of the various sacred spots were protected in the numerous risings and wars, whilst the heathen buildings also faithfully kept alive the memory of the exact position of every sanctuary venerated by the Christians. Saint Helena, the mother of Constantine, found the temples in situ; she had but to have them pulled down to discover the various Holy Places unchanged beneath their ruins.

The engraving on page 74 represents the funereal monument known as the Tomb of Absalom, no doubt because it was erected on the same spot as that formerly occupied by the tomb of the son of David. The character of the structure, however, with its mixture of Greek and Oriental details, does not justify the attribution to it of so ancient an origin. It is a chamber hewn with the chisel and the pickaxe in an isolated monolithic rock on the rising ground. The interior is entirely without ornament, but, as can be seen in the engraving, the outside is decorated with pilasters cut in the living rock, whilst the whole is surmounted by a cone added separately, part of which is also shewn in my sketch. Josephus, speaking of the original Tomb of Absalom, says that it was a marble column situated about three hundred paces from Jerusalem, and was known as Absalom's Place. This is what we read on the subject of Absalom's grave in the second book of Samuel, chap. XVIII. verse 17: « And they (the soldiers of Joab) took Absalom, and cast him into a great pit in the wood, and laid a very great heap of stones upon him: and all Israel fled every one to his tent. » Now Absalom in his life-time had erected a monument for himself in what was called the King's Dale, for he said: « I have no son to keep my name in remembrance: and he called the pillar after his own name: and it is called to this day Absalom's place. » This name is sometimes translated Absalom's Hand, which need not surprise us, for the Hebrews were in the habit of using the original word for hand to designate any special spot or to preserve its memory. It is said that everyone who passed the monument threw a stone upon it in token of the horror in which all the people of the country held Absalom's crime; and, as a matter of fact, the lower portion of the Tomb is completely hidden by the masses of stones accumulated about it.

It will, perhaps, be as well for me to call attention to the fact that I have taken this and other tombs as the starting-points of my restorations of the Temple buildings. It seemed to me natural to suppose that the architects of that period often adopted the same forms and the same style of ornamentation in their buildings, and that what we call originality now-a-days was totally unknown in that time of unchanging traditions. The artist was allowed but an infinitely small amount of liberty of design; he had but to carry out the wishes of the higher powers. Art was almost exclusively restricted to the service of religion, and was compelled not only to submit to its influence but to carry out its orders. This is self-evident in the monuments of Egyptian art which have come down to us, and Jewish art could not, of course, escape a law so general through-

The Tomb of Absalom in the Valley of Jehoshaphat.

out the East; moreover, the presence of the massive buildings dominating the Valley of Jehoshaphat would necessarily exercise a considerable influence over the imagination of the artists of the day. What better could they do than imitate the Temple? Was it not built under conditions of exceptional splendour? Was it not a sacred building, every stone of which was

North-east angle of Jerusalem.

in a certain sense a prayer? And was it not an act of piety to revive its memory in a tomb? As a result of all this a very great number of antique designs are reproduced in the works of various architects. This is why I have felt justified in introducing into some of my restorations of the Temple certain characteristic details such as the corner pediments and the cornices arranged one above the other in the peculiar manner I observed alike in the Tomb of Absalom, in that of Saint James, and in the sepulchral monuments of Petra.

Ornament in gilded metal from the Es-Sakhra Mosque, called the Mosque of Omar.

Capital from the El-Aksa Mosque

THE PASSION

HOLY THURSDAY

The Man bearing a pitcher
Saint Mark – Chap. 14

r primo die azymorum, quando pascha immolabant, dicunt ei discipuli : Quo vis eamus et paremus tibi, ut manduces pascha?

13. Et mittit duos ex discipulis suis, et dicit eis : Ite in civitatem, et occurret vobis homo lagenam aquæ bajulans; sequimini eum.

14. Et quocumque introierit, dicite domino domus, quia Magister dicit : Ubi est refectio mea, ubi pascha cum discipulis meis manducem?

The Man bearing a pitcher.

ND the first day of unleavened bread, when they killed the passover, his disciples said unto him, Where wilt thou that we go and prepare that thou mayest eat the passover?

13. And he sendeth forth two of his disciples, and saith unto them, Go ye into the city, and there shall meet you a man bearing a pitcher of water: follow him.

14. And wheresoever he shall go in, say ye to the goodman of the house, The Master saith, Where is the guestchamber, where I shall

THE PASSION

15. Et ipse vobis demonstrabit cœnaculum grande stratum, et illic parate nobis.

16. Et abierunt discipuli ejus, et venerunt in civitatem, et invenerunt sicut dixerat illis, et paraverunt pascha.

17. Vespere autem facto venit cum duodecim.

15. And he will shew you a large upper room furnished *and* prepared: there make ready for us.

16. And his disciples went forth, and came into the city and found as he had said unto them: and they made ready the passover.

17. And in the evening he cometh with the twelve.

The disciples had asked the Saviour to give them His instructions about the Passover, and He had chosen Saint Peter and Saint John to go and prepare everything, and first of all to find the place described by Him. They are represented in my picture watching for the man passing bearing a pitcher, of whom the Master had spoken, having for this purpose taken up their posts against the wall of the Sion quarter, where the street leads down by way of the Ophel suburb to the well now known as the Fountain of the Virgin, the ancient En-Rogel. The water of this well being the purest in Jerusalem was the best suited for making the unleavened bread used at the Passover. Men and women bearing pitchers pass along this street, the women in greater numbers than the men, for the fetching of water is generally their business. It would therefore be easy to observe the few men who returned from the well, slowly climbing up the hill, laden as they are with their heavy loads. Many have already passed, but not yet the one designated by the Master. When he comes, it is John, the beloved and trusted friend of Jesus, who recognizes him immediately, and the disciples at once prepare to follow him. They have scarcely a hundred steps to go, for they are already far up the street and quite close to the ancient Sion,

Jerusalem as seen from the Hill of Evil Counsel.

which looks down upon the mountain on which Jerusalem is built. The precise and homely details here given to us by the Evangelist, with those supplied throughout the whole history of the successive scenes of the Passion, enable us to obtain a wonderfully vivid and truthful idea of all the facts connected with this deeply interesting period. We feel that eye-witnesses are speaking, or at least that eye-witnesses inspired the writer even in his most minute shades of expression. Saint John saw everything, the other Apostles were in the very best possible position for obtaining trustworthy testimony; so that in reading the divine record, the whole tragic story is lived through again, as it were before our very eyes, the two thousand years which have passed roll away as though they had never been, and we receive just such a vivid impression as we should in reading a contemporary journal.

We have already, in our Introduction, given our reasons for indicating the very hours when the events we have to describe took place. To realize this idea we have adopted what seems to us the natural plan of giving the accompanying design, shewing two angels upholding a dial, to shadow forth the interest taken in Heaven from whence they come, in the work of the God-Man. They wear stoles such as are worn by priests on Good-Friday, when the sacrifice on Calvary is commemorated, and in their hands they hold tapers which are symbols of light and purity. On the dial itself the time at which the events under notice took

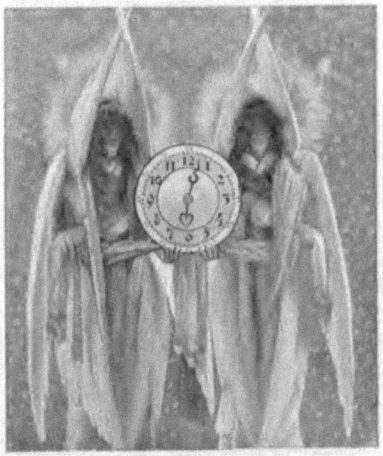

Thursday evening.

place is indicated in the modern way to make it more readily intelligible. The spectator can thus give himself up the more readily to contemplation, watch the daylight gradually die away, the moon rise, and, as it sets, see the night slowly ebb away as it were drop by drop, to give place to a new dawn, the dawn of that grand day, with its morning full of anguish, its terrible noon, its sad twilight and night. Then, face to face with the unfolding of the profoundly affecting drama, our own tears begin to flow as we, too, mark the passing of the hour. But no! that divine hour does not pass, for it is eternal! He willed to live through it: neither He nor His work can ever pass away, and He remains alive even in death. For this reason the night, symbol of eternal life, is shewn behind the angels. It is studded and illuminated by countless stars; their number and the unchanging steadfastness of their light calling up a vision of the grandeur of Him Who is about to die, and of His eternity, which has neither beginning nor end.

From the Valley of Heaven.

The Jew's Passover
Saint Matthew — Chap. 26, — v. 20

 ESPERE autem facto discumbebat cum duodecim discipulis suis.

 ow when the even was come, he sat down with the twelve.

The room is prepared for the Passover; the draperies, decorated with festoons of foliage, hang as usual between the pillars; the lamp is lit, for it is already night. The twelve Apostles, with Christ in the midst of them, are beginning the ceremonial of the feast in accordance with the ancient ritual; with robes tucked up, loins girt, sandals on the feet and the staff in the hand, in a word, in travelling dress in remembrance of the Exodus from Egypt. Thus must be accomplished the solemn ceremony every Jew was bound to perform and of which the principal rite was the eating of the Paschal Lamb.

The Lord's Supper. Judas dipping his hand in the dish.

The Lord's Supper — Judas dipping his hand in the dish
Saint Mark — Chap. 14

Espere autem facto venit cum duodecim.

18. Et discumbentibus eis et manducantibus ait Jesus : Amen dico vobis, quia unus ex vobis tradet me, qui manducat mecum.

19. At illi cœperunt contristari, et dicere ei singulatim : Numquid ego?

20. Qui ait illis : Unus ex duodecim, qui intingit mecum manum in catino.

SANCT. JOAN. — C. 13

21. Quum hæc dixisset Jesus, turbatus est spiritu, et protestatus est et dixit :

And in the evening he cometh with the twelve.

18. And as they sat and did eat, Jesus said, Verily I say unto you, One of you which eateth with me shall betray me.

19. And they began to be sorrowful, and to say unto him one by one, Is it I? and another *said*, Is it I?

20. And he answered and said unto them, *It is* one of the twelve, that dippeth with me in the dish.

SAINT JOHN. — CH. 13

21. When Jesus had thus said, he was troubled in spirit, and testified and

Amen amen dico vobis, quia unus ex vobis tradet me.

22. Aspiciebant ergo ad invicem discipuli, hæsitantes de quo diceret.

23. Erat ergo recumbens unus ex discipulis ejus in sinu Jesu, quem diligebat Jesus.

24. Innuit ergo huic Simon Petrus et dixit ei : Quis est, de quo dicit?

25. Itaque quum recubuisset ille supra pectus Jesu, dicit ei : Domine, quis est?

26. Respondit Jesus : Ille est, cui ego intinctum panem porrexero. Et quum intinxisset panem, dedit Judæ Simonis Iscariotæ.

27. Et post buccellam introivit in eum Satanas. Et dixit ei Jesus : Quod facis, fac citius.

said, Verily, verily, I say unto you, that one of you shall betray me.

22. Then the disciples looked one on another, doubting of whom he spake.

23. Now there was leaning on Jesus' bosom one of his disciples, whom Jesus loved.

24. Simon Peter therefore beckoned to him, that he should ask who it should be of whom he spake.

25. He then lying on Jesus' breast saith unto him, Lord, who is it?

26. Jesus answered, He it is, to whom I shall give a sop, when I have dipped *it*. And when he had dipped the sop, he gave *it* to Judas Iscariot, *the son* of Simon.

27. And after the sop Satan entered into him. Then said Jesus unto him, That thou doest, do quickly.

A typical Jew of Jerusalem.

We have already described the way in which the guests were placed at meals. After having removed the sandals, they ate their food reposing on couches, as indicated in the verse of the Gospel quoted above by the Latin word discumbens. This couch was a sort of divan sloping slightly towards the feet and provided with a head-rest at the upper end. Long cushions were placed on the couches so that those using them could recline comfortably on the left side, leaving the right arm and hand free. There was generally room enough on each couch for two people, except on the couches at the end of the table or on the inside of the horse-shoe it formed. The servants in waiting stood in the centre and the couches radiated all round it, each at right angles with the table. This arrangement explains how it was that Saint John, placed on the right hand of Jesus, could easily lean his head upon the breast of the Lord and speak to Him in a low voice without being heard, whilst Saint Peter, placed on the left side, had next to him the arm on which Jesus was reclining, so that it would be much more difficult for him to communicate with the Master. As for the place occupied by Judas, that is to a certain extent necessarily determined by the incident itself which is represented in my engraving: for, to be able to dip his hand in the same dish as the Saviour, he would have to occupy a seat in the centre of the horse-shoe nearly opposite to Jesus. In the Gospel account quoted above, it will be noticed how full of melancholy reproach is the insistence with which the Master speaks of the treason about to be committed. « One of the twelve », He says emphatically, so that no one may suppose He is speaking of one of the many disciples who were less familiar with His person, and on whom He had not showered so many fatherly bounties. « One of you that dippeth with me in the dish » he insists; the fact of eating out of one dish being indeed considered amongst the Jews and throughout the whole of the East as a kind of covenant, which, in case of injury inflicted by one of the parties to it on the other, aggravated the heinousness of the offence. With regard to Judas the remark had the greater weight inasmuch as he and the Lord had not taken this one meal only together, but he had long been admitted to close and constant intimacy with Jesus. Another touching detail is that the other eleven, conscious though they were of their own rectitude and of the horror with which the mere thought of betraying their Master inspired them, nevertheless asked in deep humility : « Is it I, Lord? » So profound is their confidence in the supernatural power of Jesus that they are disposed to believe in what He should say even more than in the testimony of their own consciences. It is remarkable that Jesus, Who knew beforehand which would be the traitor, behaved to Judas to the very end in a manner so full of delicate tact, that he did not feel that he was meant when he heard the simple words : « One of you shall betray me. »

Jesus washing the Disciples' feet
Saint John — Chap. 13

URGIT a cœna et ponit vestimenta sua, et quum accepisset linteum, præcinxit se.

5. Deinde mittit aquam in pelvim, et cœpit lavare pedes discipulorum et extergere linteo, quo erat præcinctus.

6. Venit ergo ad Simonem Petrum, et dicit ei Petrus : Domine, tu mihi lavas pedes?

7. Respondit Jesus et dixit ei : Quod ego facio, tu nescis modo, scies autem postea.

8. Dicit ei Petrus : Non lavabis mihi pedes in æternum. Respondit ei Jesus : Si non lavero te, non habebis partem mecum.

E riseth from supper, and laid aside his garments; and took a towel, and girded himself.

5. After that he poureth water into a bason, and began to wash the disciples' feet, and to wipe *them* with the towel wherewith he was girded.

6. Then cometh he to Simon Peter: and Peter saith unto him, Lord, dost thou wash my feet?

7. Jesus answered and said unto him, What I do thou knowest not now; but thou shalt know hereafter.

8. Peter saith unto him, Thou shalt never wash my feet. Jesus answered him, If I wash thee not, thou hast no part with me.

THE PASSION

9. Dicit ei Simon Petrus : Domine, non tantum pedes meos, sed et manus et caput.

10. Dicit ei Jesus : Qui lotus est, non indiget nisi ut pedes lavet, sed est

9. Simon Peter saith unto him, Lord, not my feet only, but also *my* hands and *my* head.

10. Jesus saith to him, He that is washed needeth not save to wash *his*

mundus totus. Et vos mundi estis, sed non omnes.

11. Sciebat enim, quisnam esset qui traderet eum; propterea dixit : Non estis mundi omnes.

feet, but is clean every whit : and ye are clean, but not all.

11. For he knew who should betray him; therefore said he, Ye are not all clean.

Their Paschal duties performed in accordance with the requirements of the Jewish law, and before the inauguration of the new rite which Jesus was about to institute, the Lord and His disciples left the room in which they had kept the Passover, to repair to another divided into two parts by a curtain, on one side of which seats were provided for the new ceremony. The Apostles were seated in the same order as before, for already the Christian hierarchy may be said to have been founded. On the left, at the edge of the table, is Judas, succeeded by Saint

Thomas, Saint Bartholomew, Saint James the Less, who is bringing the water, Saint James the Greater, and then Saint John, who is looking down at the bason in which the feet are to be washed. The Saviour has taken up His position in the centre of the group, having on His left, that is to say on the right of the picture, Saint Peter, Saint Andrew, Saint Thaddæus, Saint Simon, Saint Matthew and Saint Philip. Jesus has begun with Philip, who is putting on his sandals again; the scene with Saint Peter, described in the sacred text, will take place in the centre, and the ceremony will conclude with the washing of the feet of Judas.

The Communion of the Apostles
Saint Luke — Chap. 22

T accepto pane gratias egit, et fregit et dedit eis, dicens: Hoc est corpus meum, quod pro vobis datur;

ND he took bread, and gave thanks, and brake *it*, and gave unto them, saying, This is my body which is

hoc facite in meam commemorationem.

20. Similiter et calicem, postquam cœnavit, dicens : Hic est calix novum testamentum in sanguine meo, qui pro vobis fundetur.

given for you : this do in remembrance of me.

20. Likewise also the cup after supper, saying, This cup *is* the new testament in my blood, which is shed for you.

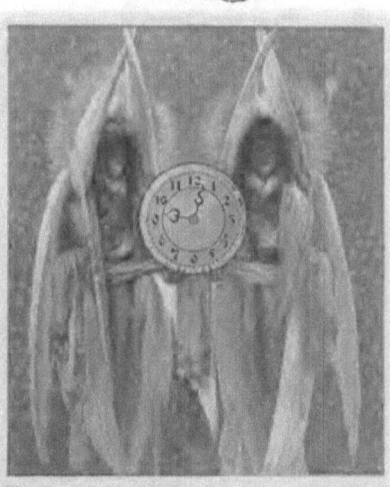

The disciples had already been profoundly moved by the washing of their feet by the Lord, and the mysterious words Jesus had just pronounced over the bread and wine had put the finishing touch to their emotion. At heart, in spite of all the comforting words their Master had lavished upon them, they are anxious and saddened by their presentiment of the events about to take place, and they are all silent. Jesus alone says a few words in a low voice: He breaks the sacred bread and distributes it amongst the disciples, who reverently approach to receive it in their hands. Such is the subject of my picture, which altogether repudiates the idea that the Eucharistic bread was passed from hand to hand, beginning with that of Jesus and ending with the most distant of the disciples, which would have made it appear as if the Apostles had not had the consolation of receiving direct in each case the token of their Master's infinite love for them. I have therefore supposed, as indeed the sacred text seems to suggest, that Saint John and Saint Peter, placed on the right and left hand of Jesus, were the first to communicate, and that the other Apostles came in turn one by one, with feelings suitable to a moment so supreme, to receive the same great privilege. The Church was now founded, and it was, therefore, fitting to inaugurate a ceremony, which was to be repeated throughout all future centuries, in such a manner as to impress all who were present with the solemnity of the sacred rite and enable them ever to retain undimmed their memory of it.

The Departure of Judas
Saint John — Chap. 13, v. 30

 cum ergo accepisset ille buccellam, exivit continuo. Erat autem nox.

 He then having received the sop went immediately out: and it was night.

Judas, impatient to execute his designs, and annoyed, moreover, at the words of Jesus : " That thou doest, do quickly », left the guest-chamber and hurried away, after having, no doubt, himself taken part in the celebration of the second Passover and received a portion of the sacred bread. It was already night and the moon was rising, casting deep shadows in the narrow streets and thus intensifying the gloom. The ninth hour was approaching, and Judas was impatiently expected. Many were those who would not go to bed that night, the gratification of their hatred would have to serve instead of repose. Complete silence reigned in the town except for the occasional barking of dogs, breaking the stillness at irregular intervals. Judas glided along the walls and went down into the city, approaching the Temple, where he expected to find the soldiers of the escort which was to go with him to take Jesus. There were some bridges to cross, and the silence seemed deeper than ever down in the valleys separating the Temple from the town. Perhaps an occasional cry may for a moment have added to the betrayer's distress; a sentinel may have fallen asleep in some porch and an officer of the night patrol may have set fire to his gibbeh or upper garment to wake him, according to the requirements of the law.

The Departure of Judas.

The last Discourse of Our Lord Jesus Christ
Saint John — Chap. 13

 cum ergo exisset, dixit Jesus : Nunc clarificatus est Filius hominis, et Deus clarificatus est in eo.

32. Si Deus clarificatus est in eo,

 Herefore, when he was gone out, Jesus said, Now is the Son of man glorified, and God is glorified in him.

32. If God be glorified in him, God

et Deus clarificabit eum in semetipso, et continuo clarificabit eum.

shall also glorify him in himself, and shall straightway glorify him.

The Last Discourse of Our Lord Jesus Christ.

33. Filioli, adhuc modicum vobiscum sum. Quæretis me, et sicut dixi Judæis : Quo ego vado, vos non potestis venire : et vobis dico modo.

34. Mandatum novum do vobis, ut diligatis invicem, sicut dilexi vos, ut et vos diligatis invicem.

35. In hoc cognoscent omnes, quia

33. Little children, yet a little while I am with you. Ye shall seek me : and as I said unto the Jews, Whither I go, ye cannot come ; so now I say to you.

34. A new commandment I give unto you, That ye love one another ; as I have loved you, that ye also love one another.

35. By this shall all *men* know that

OUR LORD JESUS CHRIST

THE LAST DISCOURSE OF OUR LORD JESUS CHRIST

discipuli mei estis, si dilectionem habueritis ad invicem.

ye are my disciples, if ye have love one to another.

SANCT. JOAN. — C. 14

SAINT JOHN — CH. 14

1. Non turbetur cor vestrum. Creditis in Deum, et in me credite.

1. Let not your heart be troubled: ye believe in God, believe also in me.

2. In domo Patris mei mansiones multæ sunt; si quo minus, dixissem vobis: Quia vado parare vobis locum.

2. In my Father's house are many mansions : if *it were* not *so*, I would have told you. I go to prepare a place for you.

3. Et si abiero et præparavero vobis locum, iterum venio et accipiam vos ad me ipsum, ut ubi sum ego et vos sitis.

3. And if I go and prepare a place for you, I will come again, and receive you unto myself; that where I am, *there* ye may be also.

4. Et quo ego vado scitis, et viam scitis.

4. And whither I go ye know, and the way ye know.

Women watching Jesus pass.

The new order had begun : the old order had already given place to it; as the Church sings in the office of the Holy Sacrament : « Et antiquum documentum novo cedat ritui. » Henceforth every act of Jesus, every gesture however slight, takes a new and, in a certain sense, a sacramental signification: it is, so to speak, the liturgical initiation of the Apostles, and it behoves them to remember in order that they may communicate to their spiritual heirs everything the Saviour did and said on this His last night on earth. In our engraving the Saviour is represented wearing His prophet's mantle, in which we see the origin of the cope, a wide garment fastened at the neck, which falls in a very different manner from an ordinary mantle. In the book of Numbers (chap. XV, v. 38) and in Deuteronomy (chap. XXII, v. 12), Moses commanded the Jews to wear at religious ceremonies a mantle adorned « with fringes upon the four quarters » and « upon the fringe of the border a ribband of blue » and a tassel made up of several bows. These four decorated corners symbolized the four letters of the name of Jehovah: J. H. V. H., and, as stated in the verse of Numbers succeeding that quoted above, those who

looked upon them were to « remember all the commandments of the Lord and do them » and not to seek after the desires of their own hearts and their own eyes which might lead them to be unfaithful. As we have already pointed out, it must have been one of these tassels that was touched by the woman with an issue of blood, when in the midst of the crowd pressing upon Him, she approached Jesus from behind in the hope of being freed from her infirmity. The stole now worn by officiating priests, with its fringes and the cross embroidered in the corners seems to us not unlike the garment we have been describing. However that may be, the Apostles are very sure to have worn the tallith with the four tassels at the Feast of the Passover, and this is why I have represented them in it in the picture illustrating the last discourse of the Lord. They are not grouped accidentally, but in strictly hierarchal order, in order to shadow forth the organization of the Church, which from this time may be looked upon as an accomplished fact. Jesus standing in the midst of His disciples, and as it were officiating for them, pronounces His last words, His farewell discourse. Reading the account of it in the Gospel of Saint John, we cannot fail to be impressed with the deep solemnity of the occasion, indeed, the whole night seems to have been passed in the observance of an uninterrupted series of sacred rites.

Ornament in gilded metal from the Es-Sakhra Mosque, called that of Omar.

« Philip, he that hath seen me hath seen the Father »

Saint John – Chap. 14

icit ei Thomas: Domine, nescimus quo vadis, et quomodo possumus viam scire?

6. Dicit ei Jesus: Ego sum via et veritas et vita; nemo venit ad Patrem, nisi per me.

7. Si cognovissetis me, et Patrem meum utique cognovissetis, et amodo cognoscetis eum et vidistis eum.

8. Dicit ei Philippus: Domine, ostende nobis Patrem, et sufficit nobis.

9. Dicit ei Jesus : Tanto tempore vobiscum sum, et non cognovistis me? Philippe, qui videt me, videt et Patrem; quomodo tu dicis : Ostende nobis Patrem?

10. Non creditis quia ego in Patre, et Pater in me est? Verba, quæ ego loquor vobis, a me ipso non loquor; Pater autem in me manens ipse facit opera.

11. Non creditis quia ego in Patre, et Pater in me est?

homas saith unto him, Lord, we know not whither thou goest; and how can we know the way?

6. Jesus saith unto him, I am the way, the truth, and the life: no man cometh unto the Father, but by me.

7. If ye had known me, ye should have known my Father also: and from henceforth ye know him, and have seen him.

8. Philip saith unto him, Lord, shew us the Father, and it sufficeth us.

9. Jesus saith unto him, Have I been so long time with you, and yet hast thou not known me, Philip? he that hath seen me hath seen the Father; and how sayest thou *then*, Shew us the Father?

10. Believest thou not that I am in the Father, and the Father in me? the words that I speak unto you I speak not of myself : but the Father that dwelleth in me, he doeth the works.

11. Believe me that I *am* in the Father, and the Father in me : or else believe me for the very works' sake.

The bridge of Kedron ; coming from Gethsemane.

12. Alioquin propter opera ipsa credite. Amen amen dico vobis, qui credit in me, opera, quæ ego facio, et ipse faciet, et majora horum faciet, quia ego ad Patrem vado.

13. Et quodcumque petieritis Patrem in nomine meo, hoc faciam, ut glorificetur Pater in Filio.

14. Si quid petieritis me in nomine meo, hoc faciam.

15. Si diligitis me, mandata mea servate.

16. Et ego rogabo Patrem, et alium Paracletum dabit vobis, ut maneat vobiscum in æternum,

17. Spiritum veritatis, quem mundus non potest accipere, quia non videt eum nec scit eum, vos autem cognoscetis eum, quia apud vos manebit et in vobis erit.

18. Non relinquam vos orphanos, veniam ad vos.

19. Adhuc modicum, et mundus me jam non videt; vos autem videtis me, quia ego vivo et vos vivetis.

20. In illo die vos cognoscetis, quia ego sum in Patre meo, et vos in me et ego in vobis.

12. Verily, verily, I say unto you, He that believeth on me, the works that I do shall he do also; and greater *works* than these shall he do; because I go unto my Father.

13. And whatsoever ye shall ask in my name, that will I do, that the Father may be glorified in the Son.

14. If ye shall ask any thing in my name, I will do *it*.

15. If ye love me, keep my commandments.

16. And I will pray the Father, and he shall give you another Comforter, that he may abide with you for ever;

17. *Even* the spirit of truth; whom the world cannot receive, because it seeth him not, neither knoweth him: but ye know him; for he dwelleth with you, and shall be in you.

18. I will not leave you comfortless: I will come to you.

19. Yet a little while, and the world seeth me no more; but ye see me: because I live, ye shall live also.

20. At that day ye shall know that I *am* in my Father, and ye in me, and I in you.

The Protestations of Saint Peter.

The Protestations of Saint Peter
Saint Matthew — Chap. 26

t hymno dicto exierunt in montem Oliveti.

31. Tunc dicit illis Jesus : Omnes vos scandalum patiemini in me in ista nocte. Scriptum est enim : Percutiam pastorem, et dispergentur oves gregis.

32. Postquam autem resurrexero, præcedam vos in Galilæam.

33. Respondens autem Petrus ait illi : Et si omnes scandalizati fuerint

ND when they had sung an hymn, they went out into the mount of Olives.

31. Then saith Jesus unto them, All ye shall be offended because of me this night: for it is written, I will smite the shepherd, and the sheep of the flock shall be scattered abroad.

32. But after I am risen again, I will go before you into Galilee.

33. Peter answered and said unto him, Though all *men* shall be offended

in te, ego numquam scandalizabor.

34. Ait illi Jesus : Amen dico tibi, quia in hac nocte, antequam gallus cantet, ter me negabis.

35. Ait illi Petrus : Etiamsi oportuerit me mori tecum, non te negabo. Similiter et omnes discipuli dixerunt.

because of thee, *yet* will I never be offended.

34. Jesus said unto him, Verily I say unto thee, That this night before the cock crow, thou shalt deny me thrice.

35. Peter said unto him, Though I should die with thee, yet will I not deny thee. Likewise also said all the disciples.

Saint Peter.

The mysterious ceremonies are now accomplished; the disciples must leave the guest-chamber and follow Jesus, Who, as is His custom, is going forth to pray. It is a very dark night: the moon appears now and then only to disappear directly, obscured by the clouds which drift across it, driven onward by the west wind from the sea. No sooner are they in the open air than the Apostles are seized with anxious forebodings, the gloomy prophecies of the Master haunt them and they feel that the terrible moment foretold is not far off. In order to reach the Garden of Gethsemane from Sion, where the guest-chamber was situated, they had to leave the town and pass the ruins of the Tower of Shiloh, but recently destroyed, and the Gate by which the refuse from the town was removed. The southern wall of the town was then skirted and, passing the Ophel Gate, they would find themselves on the slope of the mountain from which rose the huge buildings erected by Herod. In the distance, wrapt in shadow, was the bed of the Kedron torrent, at that time of year almost dried up, which was reached by a somewhat steep path dangerous at night to foot-passengers who had to cross the Kedron by a bridge. Several tombs, which still exist at the present day, were passed on the right, including those named after Absalom, Zachariah and Saint James. The whole scene is melancholy and gloomy in the extreme, for, in addition to the tombs on the left, the traveller has on the right the mighty walls of the Temple, which tower above him and almost overwhelm him with their solemn majesty. At last Jesus and His followers reach Gethsemane, the name of which means wine-press, and which was a farm or oil-press surrounded by gardens or, more strictly speaking, by orchards sacred to the cultivation of fruit-trees such as the olive, the fig and the mulberry. As they made their way thither the anxiety of the Apostles was ever on the increase as the moment of danger drew nearer, for the triple influence of the gloom of the city and of the mountain, with the growing intensity of the darkness of the night, combined to weigh down their spirits. When about half-way on the road, Saint Peter, in the enthusiasm of his faith and in his confidence in himself for the future, began to make all manner of rash protestations of fidelity, little dreaming how soon he would break his promises. As for the other disciples, they were all thoroughly unnerved by terror and they were sure to flee at the very first alarm. It is now half past ten at night.

« My soul is exceeding sorrowful unto death »
Saint Mark — Chap. 14, v. 34

T ait illis : Tristis est anima mea usque ad mortem : sustinete hic et vigilate.

ND saith unto them, My soul is exceeding sorrowful unto death : tarry ye here, and watch.

« My soul is exceeding sorrowful unto death. »

We have just explained that the Garden of Gethsemane is situated in the lower part of the valley, where begin the slopes of the Mount of Olives. Near to it are certain caves which have been converted into family tombs, some of which, as yet unoccupied, afford places of retirement for solitary prayer and meditation. After having entered the Garden with Jesus the Apostles divided into two groups: three of them following the Master at a little distance, the rest dispersing about the mountain slopes so as to watch from a somewhat higher position the approaches to the garden. From thence, in fact, they could look down upon the various paths leading up to the Temple and no one could pass along them unnoticed. The three chosen companions of Jesus: Peter, James and John, accompanied Him in the direction of the cave to which He proposed retiring, and, having reached a rock with a level surface about a stone's cast from it and a little above the path by way of which Judas and the soldiers led by him would presently appear, they halted in obedience to the command of the Saviour, whilst He Himself went slowly forward. His soul exceeding sorrowful unto death, to wrestle alone with the temptation assailing Him.

The Agony in the Garden
Saint Luke — Chap. 22

T ipse avulsus est ab eis quantum jactus est lapidis, et positis genibus orabat,

ND he was withdrawn from them about a stone's cast, and kneeled down, and prayed,

42. Dicens : Pater, si vis, transfer calicem istum a me; verumtamen non

42. Saying, Father, if thou be willing, remove this cup from me: nevertheless

The Agony in the Garden

mea voluntas, sed tua fiat.

43. Apparuit autem illi angelus de cœlo, confortans eum. Et factus in agonia prolixius orabat.

44. Et factus est sudor ejus sicut guttæ sanguinis decurrentis in terram.

not my will, but thine, be done.

43. And there appeared an angel unto him from heaven, strengthening him.

44. And being in an agony he prayed more earnestly: and his sweat was as it were great drops of blood falling down to the ground.

When Jesus had reached the cave, His anguish became even greater than before, reaching an intensity which the Evangelists describe by the expression « being in an agony ». In my

picture the Saviour is represented at the culminating moment when all the approaching sufferings of His Passion and death, aggravated by the ingratitude of mankind, rise up before Him in all their awful reality. Angels now appeared to Him, each one bringing vividly before Him

Could ye not watch with me one hour?

some one particular agony which He would have to endure; the circles they form as they move slowly about His prostrate Figure shadow forth one anguish after another with cruel relentlessness. This is the cup which Jesus prays His Father « if it be possible to remove from Him »; but all the time He knows full well that He must drink it and that to the very last drop; His soul shudders at the thought; His heart is breaking; the tears gush forth abundantly, and, in the extremity of His anguish, He falls prostrate upon the ground, whilst His features, His limbs and His garments, with the rock on which He lies, are stained with His sweat, which is « as it were great drops of blood ».

Could ye not watch with me one hour?
Saint Matthew — Chap. 26

T venit ad discipulos suos, et invenit eos dormientes, et dicit Petro : Sic non potuistis una hora vigilare mecum?

41. Vigilate et orate, ut non intretis in tentationem. Spiritus quidem promptus est, caro autem infirma.

42. Iterum secundo abiit, et oravit

ND he cometh unto the disciples, and findeth them asleep, and saith unto Peter, What, could ye not watch with me one hour?

41. Watch and pray, that ye enter not into temptation; the spirit indeed *is* willing, but the flesh *is* weak.

42. He went away again the second

THE PASSION

dicens : Pater mi, si non potest hic calix transire, nisi bibam illum, fiat voluntas tua.

time, and prayed, saying, O my Father, if this cup may not pass away from me, except I drink it, thy will be done.

After the first paroxysm of agony had subsided Jesus went to His disciples to seek for some little consolation from them. They are His dearest friends; He will tell them all He is going through, and, when they have prayed together, the force of the temptation by which He is assailed will perhaps abate. The Saviour, therefore, approaches the place where He had left them, His garments in disorder, His hair still wet with the bloody sweat, bearing witness to the awful suffering He has gone through; His whole bearing betraying the dejection in which His agony has left Him. The Apostles, worn out with sorrow and fatigue, have fallen asleep upon the rock, Peter still armed with the two swords with which he had provided himself before starting for Gethsemane. Not long ago we quoted the protestations of devotion made by the chief of the Apostles in the extremity of his zeal; his enthusiastic ardour had, however, been damped by the sad prediction of Jesus, and he had come to the garden not knowing what to think, but keeping concealed under his abayeh the two cutlasses or swords he had brought with him in case there should be a struggle. The silence and the terrors of this awful night have overcome him too now and he lies asleep, until he is roused by the gentle reproach of Jesus.

Valley of Jehoshaphat.

Judas and the multitude with swords and staves
Saint Matthew — Chap. 26, v. 47

dhuc eo loquente, ecce Judas unus de duodecim venit, et cum eo turba multa cum gladiis et fustibus, missi a principibus sacerdotum et senioribus populi.

nd while he yet spake, lo, Judas, one of the twelve, came, and with him a great multitude with swords and staves, from the chief priests and elders of the people.

"I SAW A GREAT MULTITUDE"

Iscariot, the surname of Judas, has given rise to many different opinions. Some, amongst others Eusebius and Saint Jerome, think that the traitor was born in the town of Iscarioth belonging to the tribe of Ephraim, and that he took his second name from it. Others affirm that he was of the tribe of Issachar and on that account was called Issachariotes or, abbreviated, Ischariots; but the more universally received, and certainly the most probable, explanation is that the name of the betrayer was made up of the two Hebrew words : ish and carioth or Kerioth. Now Kerioth is a small town belonging to the tribe of Judah, so that the traitor was the only one of the Apostles of Judæan extraction, the others being all from Galilee, and related more or less nearly to one family. The surname of Judas has, indeed, been variously interpreted by the commentators on the Bible, and the following are some of the meanings suggested : gloomy presentiment, the usurer, the liar, the traitor, and the leathern apron, the last in allusion to Judas having carried the bag of money. Saint Jerome translates it with the sentence : « this was his reward », and it might also mean « the man who was hanged ». The traitor and those who were with him, left Jerusalem by the same gate as Jesus Himself had done, that of Ophel; then, going down the rapid descent leading to the brook Kedron, they crossed the bridge span‑

Judas.

ning it and went on to the Garden of Gethsemane. Judas was accompanied by numerous scribes and Pharisees, and he now again exhorted them to take every possible precaution to prevent the escape of Jesus. If He attempted to slip away unperceived, as had happened before on the brow of the hill above Nazareth, or still more recently in the Temple, they must be prepared to stone Him at once! Then, however, the Master had said : « Mine hour is not yet come », whereas now the hour had come and Judas perhaps secretly wished, though he appeared to fear, the frustration of the plot his avarice had led him to engage in, but which could yield him no further advantage now. Ju‑

Thursday evening.

das was, however, to achieve complete success, and it may be that the ease with which his crime was accomplished was not the least count in his subsequent despair.

Judas betraying Jesus with a kiss
Saint Mark – Chap. 14

Ederat autem traditor ejus signum eis, dicens : Quemcumque osculatus fuero, ipse est; tenete eum et ducite caute.

And he that betrayed him had given them a token, saying, Whomsoever I shall kiss, that same is he; take him, and lead *him* away safely.

45. Et quum venisset, statim accedens ad eum ait : Ave, Rabbi, et osculatus est eum.

45. And as soon as he was come, he goeth straightway to him, and saith, Master, master ; and kissed him.

46. At illi manus injecerunt in eum, et tenuerunt eum.

46. And they laid their hands on him, and took him.

S. MATTH. c. 26

ST. MATT. CH. 26

49. Et confestim accedens ad Jesum dixit: Ave, Rabbi ; et osculatus est eum.
50. Dixitque illi Jesus : Amice, ad quid venisti? Tunc accesserunt et manus injecerunt in Jesum, et tenuerunt eum.

49. And forthwith he came to Jesus, and said, Hail, master ; and kissed him.
50. And Jesus said unto him, Friend, wherefore art thou come? Then came they, and laid hands on Jesus, and took him.

According to a tradition quoted by Saint Ignatius in a letter to Saint John the Evangelist, Saint James the Less, who was in the garden with Jesus, resembled Him so much that one might well have been taken for the other. It was, perhaps, for this reason that the Jews required of Judas that he should identify Jesus with a kiss. In my picture, Judas is seen rising *on tip-toe to reach the face of his Master. Saint Peter, seeing the treacherous embrace and anticipating the scuffle which is about to ensue, asks the Lord if he shall call the other eight Apostles, who have remained in the garden at some little distance off. The scene of the tragic incident is on the path between the Garden of Gethsemane and the Mount of Olives.*

« They went backward and fell to the ground »
Saint John — Chap. 18

ENIT illuc cum laternis et facibus et armis.

UDAS then, having received a band *of men* and officers from the chief priests and Pharisees, cometh thither with lanterns and torches and weapons.

4. Jesus itaque sciens omnia, quæ

4. Jesus therefore, knowing all things

THE PASSION

ventura erant super eum, processit et dixit eis : Quem quæritis?

5. Responderunt ei : Jesum Nazarenum. Dicit eis Jesus: Ego sum. Stabat autem et Judas, qui tradebat eum, cum ipsis.

6. Ut ergo dixit eis : Ego sum, abierunt retrorsum, et ceciderunt in terram.

7. Iterum ergo interrogavit eos: Quem quæritis? Illi autem dixerunt : Jesum Nazarenum.

8. Respondit Jesus : Dixi vobis, quia ego sum; si ergo me quæritis, sinite hos abire.

9. Ut impleretur sermo, quem dixit : Quia quos dedisti mihi, non perdidi ex eis quemquam.

that should come upon him, went forth, and said unto them, Whom seek ye?

5. They answered him, Jesus of Nazareth. Jesus saith unto them, I am *he*. And Judas also, which betrayed him, stood with them.

6. As soon then as he had said unto them, I am *he*, they went backward, and fell to the ground.

7. Then asked he them again, Whom seek ye? And they said, Jesus of Nazareth.

8. Jesus answered, I have told you that I am *he* : if therefore ye seek me, let these go their way :

9. That the saying might be fulfilled, which he spake, Of them which thou gavest me have I lost none.

Saint James the Less.

The treason is accomplished now, and from the shadows of the trees issue the satellites forming the escort of Judas, who press forward in disorder to seize the person of the Lord. The Master, seeing that they were arresting the Apostles also, exclaimed : « I am he! » and, anxious to have it fully understood that He surrendered voluntarily, He, almost for the last time before His death, availed Himself of His supernatural power. As He pronounced the simple words : « I am he! » the soldiers were all flung backward by an irresistible force and fell to the ground.

The drawing on this page represents Saint James the Less or the Small, and in this portrait I have brought out the likeness to the Master. The son of Mary Cleophas, this Apostle was one of those who were called the brothers of the Lord, because they were of the same family, and when, later, James the Less became Bishop of Jerusalem, he retained the title, which, taken in connection with his many virtues, won for him the greatest veneration even from the Jews.

Peter smites off the ear of Malchus
Saint John – Chap. 18

IMON ergo Petrus habens gladium eduxit eum, et percussit pontificis servum, et abscidit auriculam ejus dexteram. Erat autem nomen servo Malchus.

11. Dixit ergo Jesus Petro : Mitte gladium tuum in vaginam. Calicem, quem dedit mihi Pater, non bibam illum ?

HEN Simon Peter having a sword drew it, and smote the high priest's servant, and cut off his right ear. The servant's name was Malchus.

11. Then said Jesus unto Peter, Put up thy sword into the sheath : the cup which my Father hath given me, shall I not drink it ?

Peter smites off the ear of Malchus. J.-LV.

Christ healing the ear of Malchus
Saint Luke — Chap. 22

ESPONDENS autem Jesus ait : Sinite usque huc. Et quum tetigisset auriculam ejus, sanavit eum.

52. Dixit autem Jesus ad eos, qui venerant ad se, principes sacerdotum et magistratus templi et seniores : Quasi ad latronem existis cum gladiis et fustibus ?

53. Quum quotidie vobiscum fuerim in

ND Jesus answered and said, Suffer ye thus far. And he touched his ear, and healed him.

52. Then Jesus said unto the chief priests, and captains of the temple, and the elders, which were come to him, Be ye come out, as against a thief, with swords and staves ?

53. When I was daily with you in

THE PASSION

templo, non extendistis manus in me ; sed hæc est hora vestra et potestas tenebrarum.

the temple ye stretched forth no hands against me : but this is your hour, and the power of darkness.

Jesus had just been nearly strangled with barbarous brutality, and Peter, in his zeal for his Master, had used his sword, cutting off the ear of Malchus, which, covered with blood,

Christ healing the ear of Malchus.

hangs down from the head of the luckless soldier. But Jesus was there: He rebuked the too eager Apostle, and, turning to the wounded man, expressed His willingness to heal him. No doubt, think the bystanders, He is going to be guilty of some fresh act of sorcery; what a good thing it will be to have some fresh charge to add to the indictment which is being drawn up against Him whom they characterize as a deceiver. Did He not, only the other day, heal a blind man in the Temple by merely anointing his eyes with a clay made of earth mixed with His own spittle? Had He not restored to health at the Pool of Bethesda the cripple who had had an infirmity of thirty-eight years' standing? Jesus, however, troubled Himself not at all about their perverse thoughts, He touched the ear of the wounded man, and thus consecrated His last moment of liberty to the healing of one of His enemies.

« De torrente in via bibet »
Psalm 110, v. 7

 torrente in via bibet; propterea exaltabit caput.

 shall drink of the brook in the way : therefore shall he lift up the head.

According to an ancient tradition, which reappears in the visions of Anne Catherine Emmerich, Jesus, as He was passing over the Kedron bridge, on the south side of the valley, received a treacherous push by order of the Pharisees, and was flung into the torrent. The words : De torrente in via bibet were thus literally fulfilled. It is somewhat difficult to

THE BRIDGE OVER THE BROOK KEDRON

understand what object the Jews can have had in inflicting this cruel indignity on the Lord.
But they meant to bring about the death of Jesus, no matter at what cost, and, as the bridge they were crossing had no parapet, it seemed a good opportunity to get rid of Him without any noise or fuss. Had they succeeded they would have avoided a double danger. To begin with they would have averted a popular tumult, the fear of which had so much troubled the Sanhedrim at their last meeting. And then, would it not be more prudent to finish the matter off whilst the Jews had Jesus in their own power? Once let Him come into the hands of Pilate and who could say what would happen? Perhaps the false charges brought against the prisoner would seem of no account to the indifferent Roman procurator. Suppose he should set at liberty the Man Who was so fatally undermining their influence? At this thought they became capable of anything, and there would have been nothing surprising if they had bribed one of the guards, who would, of course, have had no scruples in obeying, to put their captive quietly out of the way, in such a manner that no suspicion of murder should fall upon the instigators of the crime. However that may be, the brutal action, if it were committed, must have made a vivid impression upon the mind of the traitor who was still present, already tortured as he was by remorse. We may well believe that the sad and dignified bearing of the Master as He called him « Friend » when He re-

« And they all forsook him and fled. »

ceived the kiss, succeeded by the miracle of the healing of the ear of Malchus and the supernatural falling back of the guards, must have given Judas plenty of food for reflection. Now that the ferocity of the enemies of Jesus is freely manifested and he can foresee all the consequences of his treachery, he cannot fail to be seized with terrified forebodings and to look back with horror upon the atrocious action of which he has himself been guilty.

« And they all forsook him and fled »
Saint Mark — Chap. 14, v. 50

unc discipuli ejus relinquentes eum omnes fugerunt.

SANCT. MATTH. — C. 26

56. Hoc autem totum factum est, ut adimplerentur Scripturæ prophetarum. Tunc discipuli omnes relicto eo fugerunt.

nd they all forsook him, and fled.

ST. MATTHEW — CH. 26

56. But all this was done, that the scriptures of the prophets might be fulfilled. Then all the disciples forsook him, and fled.

Saint Peter and Saint John follow afar off
Saint John – Chap. 18, v. 15

EQUEBATUR autem Jesum Simon Petrus et alius discipulus.

ND Simon Peter followed Jesus, and *so did* another disciple.

The intervention of Jesus on behalf of the Apostles at the moment of His own arrest had been successful. « If therefore ye seek me », He had said, « let these go their way ». The fact was the enemies of the Saviour knew full well that the presence of the Apostles at the trial would only embarrass the accusers, and that what they needed to support a really compromising indictment against their prisoner were trusty witnesses of a very different stamp. One disciple, however, probably Saint Mark, for he is the only Evangelist who relates the incident, and he lived at Jerusalem, was seized by the sbirri. Saint Mark tells us that the young man in question wore « a linen cloth cast about his naked body », leading us to suppose that, disturbed by the noise of the arrest and the flaring of the torches, he had run out of his house in haste just as he was. No doubt the soldiers caught hold of him by this linen cloth, and he would have been arrested had he not slipped nimbly out of it and fled from them naked, leaving the garment in the hands of his astonished captors. Not one of His friends, therefore, shared the fate of Jesus; in the very first hour, indeed, in the first moment, they all forsook Him and fled, as related in the sacred Text, illustrated by our engraving on the previous page. Not until the fatal procession had started on its way to the house of the High Priest did two of the disciples, Peter and John, regain something of their presence of mind and follow their Master afar off. Peter, no doubt, now remembered all the fine promises he had made and which he was so very soon to forget and break. As for John, the beloved disciple of Jesus, he at least was quite ready to follow Him and if need were to interfere on His behalf. Moreover, he was on good terms with the people in the house of Caiaphas, and he might well hope to be able to get in there without danger, so as to send tidings of how things were going to the other Apostles and to the Mother of Jesus, whom he had left in all the anguish of her sad forebodings. He therefore followed at some distance the multitude escorting the Master, hiding behind the low wall of the path which was very steep at that part of the way.

Saint Peter and Saint John follow afar off.

Jerusalem from the south, with Sion and the Mosques of El-Aksa and of Omar on the left.

The Via Dolorosa

HE name of Via dolorosa has been given to the road along which Jesus passed bearing His cross on leaving the Roman Prætorium, situated within the Antonia citadel, for Mount Calvary outside the Gate of Judgment, but the path followed by the Saviour from Gethsemane to the Tribunal of Caiaphas in the Sion quarter of Jerusalem, might with equal justice be called a pathway of sorrow. It is a dark and gloomy night and, though the moon is at the full, her light is so obscured by clouds that only a few pale and sickly rays make their way through them. Gethsemane, with its ancient olive trees, presents a most melancholy and impressive appearance at the bottom of the wild valley in which it is situated. The passers-by are oppressed by the dark masses rising up in every direction, especially by the frowning walls higher up upon the hill on the right. The torches of the escort do, it is true, make flashes of red light upon the surrounding darkness, but they scarcely illuminate so much as the walls of the almost perpendicular rock on which the

Thursday evening.

Temple is built. The lower portion of the ravine on the left is lost to sight in the shadows of the night, and all that can be made out at first are a few isolated tombs, whilst beyond stretches the Valley of Jehoshaphat, resembling some vast circus, with Shiloh yet farther away, gloomy enough even in the daylight, with its closely packed houses clinging as it were to the rock, but yet more dreary in the darkness, succeeded in its turn by Ophel, with the Dung gate and Sion.

Jesus taken before Annas

Saint John — Chap. 18, v. 13

 adduxerunt eum ad Annam primum; erat enim socer Caïphæ, qui erat pontifex anni illius.

 ND led him away to Annas first; for he was father-in-law to Caiaphas, which was the high priest that same year.

Jesus taken before Annas.

The first halt made by the captors of Jesus was at the house of Annas, father-in-law of Caiaphas, whose Tribunal was situated in the part of the city overlooking the so-called Millo, which they reached soon after passing through the gate. The crowd had now increased, and the populace, bribed perhaps to some extent at least by the enemies of Jesus, are already beginning to get up a tumult. All the judges have been summoned to attend and most of them are assembled in the house of Annas, a man of more importance than Caiaphas, but the law required that the case should be heard by the High-Priest of the year, and it was now decided to take Jesus to him. The procession, therefore, resumed its march and, going through an ancient gateway in the outer walls of the city, entered a network of narrow streets, where groups of hostile or merely curious spectators had already gathered. John is the only one of the Evangelists who mentions the incident of the halt at the house of Annas; the others only speak of the prisoner having been brought before Caiaphas, where the actual judgment was pronounced; they evidently considered the first pause on the road as an episode of no consequence, not worth introducing into their narrative.

The False Witnesses before Caiaphas.

The False Witnesses before Caiaphas
Saint Mark - Chap. 14

 UMMI vero sacerdotes et omne concilium quærebant adversus Jesum testimonium, ut eum morti traderent; nec inveniebant.

56. Multi enim testimonium falsum dicebant adversus eum, et convenientia testimonia non erant.

57. Et quidam surgentes falsum

 ND the chief priests and all the council sought for witness against Jesus to put him to death; and found none.

56. For many bare false witness against him, but their witness agreed not together.

57. And there arose certain, and

THE PASSION

testimonium ferebant adversus eum, dicentes :

58. Quoniam nos audivimus eum dicentem : Ego dissolvam templum hoc manu factum, et per triduum aliud non manu factum ædificabo.

59. Et non erat conveniens testimonium illorum.

60. Et exsurgens summus sacerdos in medium interrogavit Jesum, dicens : Non respondes quidquam ad ea, quæ tibi objiciuntur ab his?

61. Ille autem tacebat et nihil respondit.

bare false witness against him, saying,

58. We heard him say, I will destroy this temple that is made with hands, and within three days I will build another made without hands.

59. But neither so did their witness agree together.

60. And the high priest stood up in the midst, and asked Jesus, saying, Answerest thou nothing? what *is it* which these witness against thee?

61. But he held his peace, and answered nothing.

The crowd is increasing rapidly, swelled by the dregs of the populace of Jerusalem. A stone parapet, however, protects the Judgment Hall itself from being invaded. The latter is full : Caiaphas as President occupies an armchair in the centre, whilst the other judges, who have been purposely chosen from amongst the enemies of Jesus, are ranged in the semicircle of seats on either side. Opposite to the Presidential Chair, in the entrance indicated by two columns supporting lamps, stands Jesus bound. His hands tied together with cords, the ends of which are held by His guards. He is, in fact, quite at the mercy of the people, for the Gospel tells us that "one of the officers that stood by struck Him with the palm of the hand" at the very beginning of the trial, and neither the judges nor the Saviour's guards interfered to protect Him. The false witnesses, who have been bribed to testify against Him, can be seen rising up here and there amongst the crowd, coming to the aid of the painfully embarrassed judges, who have no accusation to bring against the pretended criminal but their own unbridled hatred. The tumult is now at its height. The air is heavy with the smoke from the lamps and the emanations from the over-excited and frenzied crowd. The judges, raising their voices, endeavour to make themselves heard above the noise, but it is just all they can do to get a hearing. Jesus alone is calm, His dignified bearing and the touching

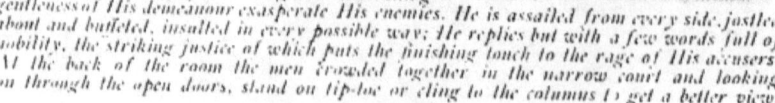

The Bridge of Kedron and the Tomb of Absalom.

gentleness of His demeanour exasperate His enemies. He is assailed from every side, jostled about and buffeted, insulted in every possible way; He replies but with a few words full of nobility, the striking justice of which puts the finishing touch to the rage of His accusers. At the back of the room the men crowded together in the narrow court and looking on through the open doors, stand on tip-toe or cling to the columns to get a better view.

Saint Peter and Saint John enter the court
THE FIRST DENIAL OF SAINT PETER
Saint John – Chap. 18

Iscipulus autem ille erat notus pontifici, et introivit cum Jesu in atrium pontificis.
16. Petrus autem stabat ad ostium foris. Exivit ergo discipulus alius, qui erat notus pontifici, et dixit ostiariæ, et introduxit Petrum.

17. Dicit ergo Petro ancilla ostiaria: Numquid et tu ex discipulis es hominis istius? Dicit ille: Non sum.

18. Stabant autem servi et ministri ad prunas, quia frigus erat, et calefaciebant se; erat autem cum eis et Petrus stans et calefaciens se.

hat disciple was known unto the high priest, and went in with Jesus into the palace of the high priest.
16. But Peter stood at the door without. Then went out that other disciple, which was known unto the high priest, and spake unto her that kept the door, and brought in Peter.

17. Then saith the damsel that kept the door unto Peter, Art not thou also *one* of this man's disciples? He saith, I am not.

18. And the servants and officers stood there, who had made a fire of coals; for it was cold: and they warmed themselves: and Peter stood with them, and warmed himself.

The second denial of Saint Peter
Saint John – Chap. 18, v. 25

rat autem Simon Petrus stans et calefaciens se. Dixerunt ergo ei: Numquid et tu ex discipulis ejus es? Negavit ille et dixit: Non sum.

SANCT. LUC. — C. 22

56. Quem quum vidisset ancilla quædam sedentem ad lumen et eum fuisset intuita, dixit: Et hic cum illo erat.

nd Simon Peter stood and warmed himself. They said therefore unto him, Art not thou also *one* of his disciples? He denied *it*, and said, I am not.

SAINT LUKE — CH. 22

56. But a certain maid beheld him as he sat by the fire, and earnestly looked upon him, and said, This man was also with him.

The second denial of Saint Peter.

57. At ille negavit cum, dicens : Mulier, non novi illum.

58. Et post pusillum alius videns eum dixit : Et tu de illis es. Petrus vero ait : O homo, non sum.

57. And he denied him, saying, Woman, I know him not.

58. And after a little while another saw him, and said, Thou art also of them. And Peter said, Man, I am not.

Annas and Caiaphas.

The High Priest rends his clothes.

The High Priest rends his clothes
Saint Matthew — Chap. 26

ESUS autem tacebat. Et princeps sacerdotum ait illi : Adjuro te per Deum vivum, ut dicas nobis, si tu es Christus Filius Dei.

64. Dicit illi Jesus : Tu dixisti ; verumtamen dico vobis : Amodo videbitis Filium hominis sedentem a dexteris virtutis Dei, et venientem in nubibus cœli.

65. Tunc princeps sacerdotum scidit vestimenta sua, dicens : Blasphemavit, quid adhuc egemus testibus?

UT Jesus held his peace. And the high priest answered and said unto him, I adjure thee by the living God, that thou tell us whether thou be the Christ, the Son of God.

64. Jesus saith unto him, Thou hast said : nevertheless I say unto you, Hereafter shall ye see the Son of man sitting on the right hand of power, and coming in the clouds of heaven.

65. Then the high priest rent his clothes, saying, He hath spoken blasphemy, what further need have we

ecce nunc audistis blasphemiam.

66. Quid vobis videtur? At illi respondentes dixerunt : Reus est mortis.

of witnesses? behold, now ye have heard his blasphemy.

66. What think ye? They answered and said, He is guilty of death.

Friday morning.

In spite of the bitter animosity of the false witnesses and the evident bias of the judges against the Accused, no distinct charge could be proved against Jesus which was not immediately upset by other testimony. Then the High Priest himself, laying aside all dignity and reserve, abandons his position as supreme judge to become himself one of the accusers. He addresses himself direct to Jesus and in so doing oversteps the rights of his office in the hope of drawing from the Prisoner a declaration which he can distort into an offence against Jehovah. Rising up in his place he adjures the Accused to bear witness against Himself. The expected reply came: « I am the Son of God », and the iniquitous High Priest at once exclaimed : « He hath spoken blasphemy », and rent his clothes. This rending of the clothes was the customary, indeed the prescribed, sign intended to mark the force of the blow struck on the heart, the intolerable anguish inflicted on the soul of a just man by hearing blasphemy. The people of the East have ever been remarkable for outward and visible expression of all emotion, which, though at first genuine and sincere enough, resulted in a whole series of ceremonial actions which in course of time degenerated into mere formalities and sometimes even into positive absurdities. At the original institution by the religious authorities of these various ceremonies, the aim of the lawgivers appears to have been to bring vividly home to each individual mind the truths these symbolic actions shadowed forth and thus intensify the feelings of which they were the expression. This is illustrated, for instance, by the way in which the Jews, worshipping in the synagogues of Jerusalem, standing with their faces to the wall and the palms of their hands turned outwards and uplifted, rise on tip-toe to symbolize the elevation of their soul towards God. In the same way, when chanting the Psalm De Profundis, the chorister, the better to mark the meaning of the words : « Out of the depths, oh Lord, I cry unto thee », stands in a deep hole dug in the earth. It was expected as a matter of course that every good Israelite who heard a blasphemy should rend his garments, and in course of time this Pharisaical ceremony had become quite ridiculous. A small knife was hung from the waistband with which the operation was performed, and a slit a few inches long cut in the mantle and lightly caught together again, rendered it yet more easy. The Rabbis, who delighted in such puerile details, had drawn up a whole code of rules on the subject. The rent in the garments must be made standing, it must, moreover, be in the front of the robe, starting from the neck and on no account from the fringe. Furthermore, the rent must be a hand's breadth long and must be made in all the garments, of which ten were generally worn, except in that next the skin and in the tallith (Maimonides). Of course, in a court of justice the rending of his garments by the judge was but a feint intended to impose on the spectators, or perhaps it was merely meant to shadow forth in a tangible way the judgment about to be pronounced.

The Lord turned and looked upon Peter

THE THIRD DENIAL

Saint Luke – Chap. 22

Et intervallo facto quasi horæ unius, alius quidam affirmabat dicens : Vere et hic cum illo erat; nam et Galilæus est.

60. Et ait Petrus : Homo, nescio quid dicis. Et continuo adhuc illo loquente cantavit gallus.

61. Et conversus Dominus respexit Petrum. Et recordatus est Petrus verbi Domini, sicut dixerat : Quia priusquam gallus cantet, ter me negabis.

And about the space of one hour after another confidently affirmed, saying, Of a truth this *fellow* also was with him : for he is a Galilæan.

60. And Peter said, Man, I know not what thou sayest. And immediately, while he yet spake, the cock crew.

61. And the Lord turned, and looked upon Peter. And Peter remembered the word of the Lord, how he had said unto him, Before the cock crow, thou shalt deny me thrice.

The Valley of Jehoshaphat, coming from Bethany. J.J.T.

In spite of his repeated denials, Peter approached the Judgment Hall to try to see what was going on, whilst Saint John thus left to himself had availed himself of his own special facilities to secure a place as near as possible to Jesus. Peter, finding himself surrounded on all sides by strangers, for as a Galilean he was, of course, a foreigner, and attracted the constant notice of the guards by his peculiar accent, became nervous, lost his presence of mind and, getting more and more over-excited, he denied his Master for the third time. The man referred to by Saint Luke, though he does not mention his name, was perhaps the kinsman of Malchus, of whom Saint John speaks in his account of the same scene ; or it may even have been the same person who Saint Matthew relates said to Peter «thou also art one of them, for thy speech bewrayeth thee». It is, however, very possible that each of the three men mentioned was a different person, and that Peter did not utter his false oaths until he was absolutely driven to do so by the

harassing attacks made on him from every side. Saint Mark seems to sanction this interpretation of the denier's conduct, by attributing to several different persons the questions the other Evangelists appear to put into the mouth of one man only. They that stood by said again to Peter. Surely thou art one of them : « for thou art a Galilean and thy speech agreeth thereto. » When the scene represented in my picture took place, the trial was over, the sentence had been pronounced, and the judges were retiring. It is late, about three o'clock, and the cock crows again. Jesus is leaving the Judgment Hall, given over for a few moments to the tumultuous mob, intoxicated with fury against Him which has been surging about the scene of the trial for nearly four hours. He is being taken, subjected the while to the most cruel treatment, to a small prison adjoining the Judgment Hall where He is to be kept in sight by His guards for the rest of the night, and it is in this short transit that Jesus turns round and looks upon Peter. It would indeed be difficult to analyze all that look expressed; but Peter himself understood it all too well, that rapid glance lights up his troubled conscience like a flash of lightning in the night,

Jesus turned and looked upon Peter.

and suddenly everything comes back to his memory : his protestations on the way to Gethsemane, the warnings of Jesus, his own thrice-repeated denial and the crowing of the cock.

Christ buffeted and mocked in the House of Caiaphas
Saint Matthew — Chap. 26

 Tunc exspuerunt in faciem ejus et colaphis eum ceciderunt; alii autem palmas in faciem ejus dederunt,

68. Dicentes : Prophetiza nobis, Christe, quis est qui te percussit?

SANCT. MARC. — C. 14

65. Et cœperunt quidam conspuere eum et velare faciem ejus et colaphis eum cædere, et dicere ei : Prophe-

 Then did they spit in his face, and buffeted him; and others smote *him* with the palms of their hands,

68. Saying, Prophesy unto us, thou Christ, Who is he that smote thee?

SAINT MARK — CH. 14

65. And some began to spit on him, and to cover his face, and to buffet him, and to say unto him, Prophesy :

CHRIST MOCKED IN THE HOUSE OF CAIAPHAS

CHRIST BUFFETED AND MOCKED IN THE HOUSE OF CAIAPHAS

tiza; et ministri alapis eum cædebant.

SANCT. LUC. — C. 22

63. Et viri, qui tenebant illum, illudebant ei cædentes.

64. Et velaverunt eum et percutiebant faciem ejus, et interrogabant eum, dicentes : Prophetiza, quis est qui te percussit?

65. Et alia multa blasphemantes dicebant in eum.

and the servants did strike him with the palms of their hands.

SAINT LUKE — CH. 22

63. And the men that held Jesus mocked him, and smote him.

64. And when they had blindfolded him, they struck him on the face, and asked him, saying, Prophesy, who is it that smote thee?

65. And many other things blasphemously spake they against him.

The subject now represented takes us back to a little before the third denial of Peter, or at least to before the Lord turned and looked at him, for we assume that the look was given on the way to prison. Jesus once condemned by acclamation on the suggestion of the High Priest himself, a nameless scene of horror began. The Sanhedrim, instead of protecting Him from the crowd, as in such a case it was the duty of the legal authorities to do, abandoned Him to their mercy and thus sanctioned the worst outrages. It is true that the members of the Supreme Council did not themselves take any part in the insults heaped on Jesus, but there is not the slightest doubt that they were as responsible as if they had, for they certainly could have prevented them. His persecutors flung themselves upon the Prisoner with a positively diabolical fury, raining blows upon Him. « spitting in His face, buffeting Him and smiting Him with the palms of their hands. » They blindfolded Him with a dirty rag, and as they struck Him they mocked Him, saying : « Prophesy unto us, thou Christ, who is he that smote thee? » Truly the unfortunate Victim paid dearly enough now for His brief triumph on Palm Sunday, for the homage paid to Him at Bethany, for the precious ointment of Mary Magdalene and for His few short moments of joy, which He must now expiate with all this agony and humiliation. The enemies of the Prophet cannot but have been intoxicated with the thought of having Him, Who had previously caused them so much anxiety, in their hands under such conditions. But the night was far spent, even the tormentors were getting weary, and there was no longer any danger of the escape of their Victim. The crowd now melted away and the guards led Jesus, with soiled garments, bleeding face, and limbs bruised by the blows He had received and galled by His fetters, as He had now been bound some four hours, it being already three o'clock in the morning, that is to say, eleven hours since He was taken prisoner. Long before, Job had said, and his words were perhaps prophetic of the sufferings of Christ : « They have gaped upon me with their mouth, they have smitten me upon the cheek reproachfully; they have gathered themselves together against me. » These words were literally fulfilled in the scene we have just described, and yet more remarkably true was the beautifully worded prophecy of Isaiah, when he glorified beforehand the divine gentleness of the insulted Messiah, saying : « I gave my back to the smiters, and my cheeks to them that plucked off the hair: I hid not my face from shame and spitting. »

The cock crew
Saint Luke — Chap. 22, v. 60

T ait Petrus : Homo, nescio quid dicis. Et continuo adhuc illo loquente cantavit gallus.

S. MARC. — C. 14

72. Et statim gallus iterum cantavit. Et recordatus est Petrus verbi, quod dixerat ei Jesus : Priusquam gallus cantet bis, ter me negabis.

S. MATTH. — C. 26

74. Tunc cœpit detestari et jurare, quia non novisset hominem. Et continuo gallus cantavit.

ND Peter said, Man, I know not what thou sayest. And immediately, while he yet spake, the cock crew.

SAINT MARK — CH. 14

72. And the second time the cock crew. And Peter called to mind the word that Jesus said unto him, Before the cock crow twice, thou shalt deny me thrice. And when he thought thereon, he wept.

ST. MATTH. — CH. 26

74. Then began he to curse and to swear, *saying*, I know not the man. And immediately the cock crew.

Peter went out and wept bitterly.

Peter went out and wept bitterly
Saint Luke — Chap. 22, v. 62

T egressus foras Petrus flevit amare.

SANCT. MATTH. — C. 26

75. Et recordatus est Petrus verbi Jesu, quod

ND Peter went out, and wept bitterly.

ST. MATTH. — CH. 26

75. And Peter remembered the word of Jesus,

dixerat : Priusquam gallus cantet, ter me negabis. Et egressus foras flevit amare.

which said unto him, Before the cock crow, thou shalt deny me thrice. And he went out, and wept bitterly.

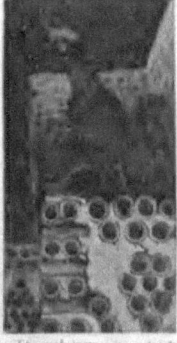

The cock crew.

In Syria the cocks are heard crowing for the first time between eleven o'clock and midnight, they crow the second time between one and two o'clock, and that with the punctuality of a clock, whilst the third crowing takes place about three o'clock in the morning. Now it was about the third watch of the night, that is to say, towards three o'clock in the morning, that Jesus left the Judgment Hall to be taken to prison where He was to remain until daybreak, waiting for the second judgment, which was to endorse officially the one already pronounced upon the Prisoner during the night. It came about, therefore, quite naturally for the third and last crowing of the cock to coincide with the look of reproach from Jesus and combine to trouble the soul of Saint Peter and produce an agonized burst of remorseful repentance. Outside the Judgment Hall groups of bystanders had probably collected at the beginning of the remarkable scenes which had taken place. In Eastern countries, where neighbours visit each other so readily, the news of what was going on would spread round about with great rapidity, and everyone from far and near would hasten to see what was going to happen. Moreover, the friends of Jesus, the Holy Women especially, could not have been indifferent to His fate: they are very sure to have been there, anxiously on the watch in the hope of some chance occurring of seeing Him, hearing Him speak and getting some idea, if only from a distance, of how things were going with Him. No doubt they were aware of the presence in the Palace of Caiaphas of Peter and of John, and they must indeed have impatiently waited for them to come out to give them some account of what had happened. Presently the uproar within became greater than ever, the yelling of the crowd could be more distinctly heard; for the sitting of the Council was coming to an end. Then the door opened quite suddenly, and Peter, beside himself with grief, rushed out weeping bitterly. The friends of the Lord surrounded him, asking questions and trying to find out from him what was to become of Jesus. Through his sobs Peter manages to make them understand that the Master is condemned to death, and that he, the chief of His Apostles, has denied Him three times. Then Peter left them, to take his way with tottering steps down into the valley, and, leaving the town, to join the rest of the disciples, who were no doubt still hidden in the caves of the Valley of Hinnom

Friday morning.

GOOD FRIDAY

The morning. — Jesus in prison

T confestim mane consilium facientes summi sacerdotes cum senioribus et scribis et universo concilio, vincientes Jesum duxerunt et tradiderunt Pilato.

SANCT. MARC. — C. 15, V. 1

ND straightway in the morning the chief priests held a consultation with the elders and scribes and the whole council, and bound Jesus, and carried *him* away, and delivered *him* to Pilate.   ST. MARK — CH. 15, V. 1

Friday morning Jesus in prison

The tumult is over now for a time and Jesus, still bound, is alone in prison. The pale white light of the dawn already heralds the opening of the much longed-for day. The Saviour is engaged in prayer, and is offering up to His Father the day which is to be so pregnant of results and for which, to quote His own words, He is come. We have represented Him bound to a short column, and certain slight marks on it lead us to suppose that that column is the very one still preserved in the Church of Saint Praxedes at Rome. Every Court of Justice had its scourging column, but probably the form differed considerably. Saint Jerome tells us that he saw the Column of the Scourging in the porch of a church at Sion; some fragments of this Column are reverently preserved in the Church of the Holy Sepulchre at Jerusalem and others in various sanctuaries of Europe: at Madrid, Venice, and elsewhere. The Column, which is now at Rome, was taken there six hundred years after the time of Jerome, that is to say, in the tenth century, a fact which must be borne in mind in considering the authenticity of the various relics. As for us, we have come to the conclusion after due consideration of the facts we have to judge by, that Jesus was bound at different times to three different columns; that connected with the Judgment Hall of Caiaphas; that of the actual scourging, and that of the crowning with thorns. We have already said where the first two now are and add here that the third is in the Church of the Holy Sepulchre at Jerusalem.

The Judgment on the morning of Good Friday
Saint Luke – Chap. 22

Et ut factus est dies, convenerunt seniores plebis, et principes sacerdotum et scribæ, et duxerunt illum in concilium suum, dicentes : Si tu es Christus, dic nobis.

67. Et ait illis : Si vobis dixero, non credetis mihi;

68. Si autem et interrogavero, non respondebitis mihi, neque dimittetis.

69. Ex hoc autem erit Filius hominis sedens a dexteris virtutis Dei.

70. Dixerunt autem omnes : Tu ergo es Filius Dei? Qui ait : Vos dicitis, quia ego sum.

71. At illi dixerunt : Quid adhuc desideramus testimonium? ipsi enim audivimus de ore ejus.

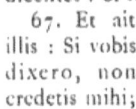ND as soon as it was day, the elders of the people and the chief priests and the scribes came together, and led him into their council, saying,

67. Art thou the Christ? tell us. And he said unto them, If I tell you, ye will not believe :

68. And if I also ask *you*, ye will not answer me, nor let *me* go.

69. Hereafter shall the Son of man sit on the right hand of the power of God.

70. Then said they all, Art thou then the Son of God? And he said unto them, Ye say that I am.

71. And they said, What need we any further witness? for we ourselves have heard of his own mouth.

The Judgment on the morning of Good Friday

Judas repents and returns the price of blood
Saint Matthew — Chap. 27

T vinctum adduxerunt eum et tradiderunt Pontio Pilato præsidi.

ND when they had bound him, they led *him* away, and delivered him to Pontius Pilate the governor.

3. Tunc videns Judas, qui cum tradidit, quod damnatus esset, pœnitentia ductus retulit triginta argenteos principibus sacerdotum et senioribus,

4. Dicens: Peccavi tradens sanguinem justum. At illi dixerunt: Quid ad nos? tu videris.

5. Et projectis argenteis in templo recessit, et abiens laqueo se suspendit.

6. Principes autem sacerdotum acceptis argenteis dixerunt: Non licet eos mittere in corbonam, quia pretium sanguinis est.

7. Consilio autem inito emerunt ex illis agrum figuli in sepulturam peregrinorum.

8. Propter hoc vocatus est ager ille

3. Then Judas, which had betrayed him, when he saw that he was condemned, repented himself, and brought again the thirty pieces of silver to the chief priests and elders.

4. Saying, I have sinned in that I have betrayed the innocent blood. And they said, What *is that* to us? see thou *to that*.

5. And he cast down the pieces of silver in the temple, and departed, and went and hanged himself.

6. And the chief priests took the silver pieces, and said, It is not lawful for to put them into the treasury, because it is the price of blood.

7. And they took counsel, and bought with them the potter's field, to bury strangers in.

8. Wherefore that field was called,

Judas repents and returns the price of blood.

JUDAS REPENTS AND RETURNS THE PRICE OF BLOOD

Haceldama, hoc est, ager sanguinis, usque in hodiernum diem.

The field of blood, unto this day.

9. Tunc impletum est quod dictum est per Jeremiam prophetam, dicentem: Et acceperunt triginta argenteos pretium appretiati, quem appretiaverunt a filiis Israel,

The Valley of Hinnom (Aceldama).

9. Then was fulfilled that which was spoken by Jeremy the prophet, saying, And they took the thirty pieces of silver, the price of him that was valued, whom they of the children of Israel did value;

10. Et dederunt eos in agrum figuli, sicut constituit mihi Dominus.

10. And gave them for the potter's field, as the Lord appointed me.

It is still early morning. Jesus has just heard the ratification of His sentence and that it was decided He should be taken before the Roman Governor. Then Judas, " which had betrayed Him ", when he sees that his Victim cannot possibly escape death, realizes at last the full extent of his treacherous wrong-doing, and his soul is seized with remorse. He repents, but his repentance is the repentance of despair, and, eager to get rid of the torture which overwhelms him, he hastens to the Temple, determined to confess his crime and to give back the money he had received on the evening of the day before. The Jews are in the Temple, wearing on their foreheads the phylacteries always put on for morning prayer. If, however, the miserable man had had any hope that the step he was about to take would save Jesus, the revolting reply he received must very quickly have convinced him of his mistake. Then his despair reaches its height, he flings down the pieces of silver in a great hurry and rushes away to go and kill himself. We have laid the scene of this tragic incident in the Court of the Jews in the lower part of the Temple.

Friday morning.

Judas hangs himself
Saint Matthew — Chap. 27, v. 5

T projectis argenteis in templo recessit, et abiens laqueo se suspendit.

ND he cast down the pieces of silver in the temple, and departed, and went and hanged himself.

Judas hangs himself

ACTUS APOST.
C. I

16. Viri fratres, oportet impleri Scripturam, quam prædixit Spiritus sanctus per os David de Juda, qui fuit dux eorum, qui comprehenderunt Jesum.

17. Qui connumeratus erat in nobis, et sortitus est sortem ministerii hujus.

18. Et hic quidem possedit agrum de mercede iniquitatis, et suspensus crepuit medius, et diffusa sunt omnia viscera ejus.

ACTS OF THE APOSTLES
CH. I

16. Men *and* brethren, this scripture must needs have been fulfilled, which the Holy Ghost by the mouth of David spake before concerning Judas, which was guide to them that took Jesus.

17. For he was numbered with us, and had obtained part of this ministry.

18. Now this man purchased a field with the reward of iniquity; and falling headlong, he burst asunder in the midst, and all his bowels gushed out.

Origen represents Judas as having hastened to kill himself so as to reach the Abode of the Departed before his Master, that he might beseech Him to have mercy upon him. Lightfoot, on the other hand, makes out that the traitor was seized by the devil, who strangled him in the air and then let his body fall to the ground. As a matter of fact, the death of the betrayer was a more simple matter, and it is enough to accept literally what Saint Peter says on the subject in the Acts of the Apostles (chap. 1, v. 18): « And falling headlong, he burst asunder in the midst, and all his bowels gushed out. » According to tradition this last crime was committed in a lonely corner of the Valley of Jehoshaphat near the village of Shiloh.

The Apostles hiding in the Valley of Hinnom.

The Apostles hiding in the Valley of Hinnom

Tradition justifies us in forming a very distinct picture of how the Apostles behaved after they had left their Master. It appears pretty certain that they left Gethsemane by way of the lower portion of the valley, keeping alongside of the bed of the Kedron torrent, passing the tombs which rose up on their right and then, finding that they were not pursued, they halted to consult together as to where they should go, deciding in the end to direct their steps towards the sepulchral caves of the Valley of Hinnom. There they would be quite safe from surprise, not too far from the town, and at the same time they would be not so very distant from Sion, so that they might hope to receive news of their Master. This Valley of Hinnom, on the south of Jerusalem, separates the tribes of Benjamin and of Judah from each other. On the west it becomes merged in the Valley of Gihon and on the south it adjoined the King's Garden, watered by the Pool of Siloam. In former times, under the earlier kings, who reigned before Josiah, as already related, sacrifices were offered up to Moloch in this valley, and it was called the Valley of Tophet or of the Drums, because those musical instruments were beaten to drown the cries of the unfortunate children offer-

Valley of Hinnom with its ancient tombs where the Apostles hid themselves.

ed up to the god. « Therefore », to quote the Prophet Jeremiah (chap. VII, v. 32), « behold the days shall come, saith the Lord, that it shall no more be called Tophet nor the valley of the son of Hinnom but the valley of slaughter, for they shall bury in Tophet till there be no places. As a matter of fact the southern side of this valley is full of tombs hewn in the living rock, and it is amongst them that tradition tells us the Apostles took refuge after Jesus had been arrested in the Garden of Gethsemane. One of these isolated tombs, which is among the first the traveller comes to at the bottom of the valley, is in fairly good preservation, and from it we may gain an idea of the original appearance of the tomb of our blessed Lord. It is entered by a vestibule in the same manner as is the Church of the Holy Sepulchre, and part of it is detached from the mountain, whilst the rest is hollowed out beneath it. The style of the various tombs corresponds with that of most of the architecture of the country; that is to say, with Greek architecture in its decadence, with an Egyptian moulding surmounting the whole. The cornice is generally enriched with triglyphs which separate from each other medallions and bunches of grapes, the latter a very favourite ornament with Jewish architects. The limestone rock of which the mountain is here built up, lends itself very readily to the excavation of these tombs and the fine grain of the stone is at the same time suitable for the carving of the various decorative details. Though it is easily worked when it is being hewn or carved it rapidly becomes sufficiently hardened on exposure to the action of the air and light to give to the sculptures produced in it considerable durability.

Jesus led from Caiaphas to Pilate
Saint Matthew — Chap. 27, v. 2

T vinctum adduxerunt eum et tradiderunt Pontio Pilato præsidi.

ND when they had bound him, they led *him* away and delivered him to Pontius Pilate the governor.

SANCT. JOAN. — C. 18

28. Adducunt ergo Jesum a Caipha in prætorium. Erat autem mane, et ipsi non introierunt in prætorium, ut non contaminarentur, sed ut manducarent Pascha.

SAINT JOHN — CH. 18

28. Then led they Jesus from Caiaphas unto the hall of judgment: and it was early; and they themselves went not into the judgment hall, lest they should be defiled; but that they might eat the passover.

The crowds accompanying Jesus now all hastened down the steep streets leading from the Sion to the Roman quarter of the town where the Prætorium was situated. There, in the Antonia Citadel, dwelt Pilate the Governor, and in it also were the barracks of the Roman garrison. Jesus has been stripped of the garments He had worn when He had left the guest-chamber the evening before. They were much soiled, and bore witness all too clearly to the cruel treatment to which their wearer had been subjected during the night: if the Governor had seen them he might have turned their condition to the advantage of the prisoner, for he might have chosen to consider the state they were in as an insult to his own dignity, as well as an outrage on humanity. Jesus therefore wore nothing now but his seamless undergarment and the rest of His clothes, which were of a reddish colour, were not restored to Him until just before He was compelled to carry His cross. — The procession went down the Tyropœon valley which was crossed by means of bridges. It was then a very deep depression, completely separating the Temple from the town, but it became

The greater part of the supposed site of the Temple.

filled up in the various subsequent sieges. The crowds which had collected the evening before were now augmented by a fresh concourse of people; the judges before whom Jesus had been taken in the morning were hastening along on their asses with their scribes to be present at the examination by the Governor. They stand in great dread of the Roman representative, for the contempt with which he treats them on every fresh opportunity does not tend to inspire them with confidence, and they feel that they must be on the spot to accuse Jesus and if need be to rouse up the people and incite them to demand the death of Him they have themselves

already condemned. — The weather is now overcast, a slight rain fell in the morning and still continues to fall at intervals, the road is slippery and many fall by the way. Jesus Himself is wet through. In the lower quarters of the town where the people had been aroused during the night by the tumult which had been going on, the excitement and disorder have begun, and everyone is already flocking in the direction of the Antonia Citadel, where the events of the new day are to be inaugurated.

Jesus before Pilate for the first time
Saint John – Chap. 18

XIVIT ergo Pilatus ad eos foras, et dixit : Quam accusationem affertis adversus hominem hunc?

30. Responderunt et dixerunt ei : Si

ILATE then went out unto them, and said, What accusation bring ye against this man?

30. They answered and said unto him,

Jesus before Pilate for the first time.

non esset hic malefactor, non tibi tradidissemus eum.

31. Dixit ergo eis Pilatus : Accipite eum vos et secundum legem vestram judicate eum. Dixerunt ergo ei Judæi : Nobis non licet interficere quemquam.

32. Ut sermo Jesus impleretur, quem dixit significans, qua morte esset moriturus.

33. Introivit ergo iterum in prætorium Pilatus, et vocavit Jesum et dixit ei : Tu es rex Judæorum?

34. Respondit Jesus : A temetipso hoc dicis, an alii dixerunt tibi de me?

35. Respondit Pilatus : Numquid ego Judæus sum? Gens tua et pontifices tradiderunt te mihi ; quid fecisti?

If he were not a malefactor, we would not have delivered him up unto thee.

31. Then said Pilate unto them, Take ye him, and judge him according to your law. The Jews therefore said unto him, It is not lawful for us to put any man to death :

32. That the saying of Jesus might be fulfilled, which he spake, signifying what death he should die.

33. Then Pilate entered into the judgment hall again, and called Jesus, and said unto him, Art thou the King of the Jews?

34. Jesus answered him, Sayest thou this thing of thyself, or did others tell it thee of me?

35. Pilate answered, Am I a Jew? Thine own nation and the chief priests have delivered thee unto me : what hast thou done?

THE PASSION

36. Respondit Jesus: Regnum meum non est de hoc mundo; si ex hoc mundo esset regnum meum, ministri mei utique decertarent, ut non traderer Judæis; nunc autem regnum meum non est hinc.

37. Dixit itaque ei Pilatus: Ergo rex es tu? Respondit Jesus: Tu dicis, quia rex sum ego. Ego in hoc natus sum et ad hoc veni in mundum, ut testimonium perhibeam veritati; omnis qui est ex veritate, audit vocem meam.

38. Dicit ei Pilatus: Quid est veritas? Et quum hoc dixisset, iterum exivit ad Judæos et dicit eis: Ego nullam invenio in eo causam.

36. Jesus answered, My kingdom is not of this world: if my kingdom were of this world, then would my servants fight, that I should not be delivered to the Jews: but now is my kingdom not from hence.

37. Pilate therefore said unto him, Art thou a king then? Jesus answered, Thou sayest that I am a king. To this end was I born, and for this cause came I into the world, that I should bear witness unto the truth. Every one that is of the truth heareth my voice.

38. Pilate saith unto him, What is truth? And when he had said this, he went out again unto the Jews, and saith unto them, I find in him no fault *at all*.

A corner of the Haram.

Pilate.

As we have already just stated, Jesus was clothed during part of His Passion with nothing more than the seamless under-garment of a brownish-red colour which had been woven by His mother. The early painters of Christian subjects represented Jesus clothed in this garment, which they made of a violet or reddish hue, with the result that people came to the conclusion that the Saviour was in the habit of wearing a red robe and, as everyone knew that He had some blue in His costume, for the corners of the tallith or sacred mantle which all Jews wore in the Synagogue and in the Temple had to be blue, it became customary to supplement the red garment of Christ with a blue mantle. There can, however, be no doubt that this was not according to the facts of the case; Jesus must have worn white robes, such as those of the Levites and of the various members of the priesthood. He. Who was as innocent as the very light itself, could not have worn red, which amongst the Jews was looked upon as the symbol of sin. We have already alluded to this fact in speaking of the garments worn by Mary Magdalene, and if objection to what we are saying is urged on the ground of the words of Isaiah (ch. LXIII, v. 2) : « Wherefore art thou red in thine apparel? » it is quite easy to reply that this refers to the blood with which the raiment of Christ was stained, or at the very most to that moment of His Passion when He was deprived of His white outer garments. In the preceding section of this work, we alluded to the fact mentioned in the Gospel of Saint John (ch. XVIII, v. 28), that the Jews went not themselves into the Judgment Hall, lest they should be defiled and be thereby prevented from eating the Passover. This explains how it was that when Pilate wished to confer with the Jews he « went forth » to speak to them, returning again to Jesus, with Whom he thus found himself alone. The Hall of Audience in the Prætorium was on the first floor, and its height can still be exactly estimated by

Friday morning.

means of the twenty-eight white marble steps which led up to it and were carried away by Saint Helena, to be eventually preserved in the Church of Santa Croce di Gerusalemme, at Rome. The room in question adjoined a loggia which served as a kind of tribune to the Governor, when, as sometimes happened, he took it into his head to harangue the people. To go backwards and forwards from it to the room in which Jesus was involved, therefore, the taking by Pilate of but a very few steps. All the local arrangements represented in my various pictures were suggested to me by one or another passage in the Gospel narrative, which throws a very vivid light on the subject for those who read it attentively.

Frieze from a Tomb in the Valley of Hinnom.

The Message from Pilate's Wife
Saint Matthew – Chap. 27, v. 19

EDENTE autem illo pro tribunali, misit ad eum uxor ejus, dicens : Nihil tibi et justo illi : multa enim passa sum hodie per visum propter eum.

HEN he was set down on the judgment seat, his wife sent unto him, saying, Have thou nothing to do with that just man : for I have suffered many things this day in a dream because of him.

The Message from Pilate's Wife

Pilate has left the Prætorium to parley with the Jews who are waiting below opposite the loggia. He is seated in a movable chair of state raised on several steps as a sign of his high rank and power. A servant hastens in, bringing a message from his wife, whose name, according to tradition, was Claudia Procula or Procla. The servant brings with her the ring of her mistress as a proof of the authenticity of the message. The noble, touching tenour of this message *shews that Procla has a soul worthy of conversion to Christianity; so that it is by no means difficult to believe that she did become, as tradition relates, a follower of the Saviour. The Greek menology even goes so far as to place her in the rank of the Saints, and certain legends relate that Pilate, who was always alike ambitious and irresolute, persecuted her to such an extent that she left him to join the Christian community.*

Jesus before Herod
Saint Luke – Chap. 23

T autem Pilatus ad principes sacerdotum et turbas : Nihil invenio causæ in hoc homine.

HEN said Pilate to the chief priests and to the people, I find no fault in this man.

JESUS BEFORE HEROD

5. At illi invalescebant, dicentes: Commovet populum, docens per universam Judæam, incipiens a Galilæa usque huc.

6. Pilatus autem audiens Galilæam, interrogavit si homo Galilæus esset.

7. Et, ut cognovit, quod de Herodis potestate esset, remisit eum ad Herodem, qui et ipse Jerosolymis erat illis diebus.

8. Herodes autem viso Jesu gavisus est valde; erat enim cupiens ex multo tempore videre eum, eo quod audierat multa de eo, et sperabat signum aliquod videre ab eo fieri.

9. Interrogabat autem eum multis sermonibus. At ipse nihil illi respondebat.

10. Stabant autem principes sacerdo-

5. And they were the more fierce, saying, He stirreth up the people, teaching throughout all Jewry, beginning from Galilee, to this place.

6. When Pilate heard of Galilee, he asked whether the man were a Galilæan.

7. And as soon as he knew that he belonged unto Herod's jurisdiction, he sent him to Herod, who himself also was at Jerusalem at that time.

8. And when Herod saw Jesus, he was exceeding glad: for he was desirous to see him of a long *season*, because he had heard many things of him; and he hoped to have seen some miracle done by him.

9. Then he questioned with him in many words; but he answered him nothing.

10. And the chief priests and scribes

Jesus before Herod.

THE PASSION

tum et scribæ constanter accusantes eum.

11. Sprevit autem illum Herodes cum exercitu suo, et illusit indutum veste alba, et remisit ad Pilatum.

stood and vehemently accused him.

11. And Herod with his men of war set him at nought, and mocked *him*, and arrayed him in a gorgeous robe, and sent him again to Pilate.

The decision of Pilate to send Jesus back to Herod appears to have had a twofold motive; in the first place he wished to get rid of a galling responsibility, and in the second he wished to pay his court to Herod, with whom, as the sacred text implies, he was at enmity. There were in fact many causes of friction between the governor of Judæa and the tetrarch of Galilee. The various feasts which took place at Jerusalem often led to risings, in which the men of Galilee always took the most prominent part; they were, therefore, generally the first to fall victims

Jerusalem and Shiloh.

to the vengeance of the pro-consul, and more often than not their own Sovereign may have considered the means of repression resorted to excessive. In Saint Luke, ch. XIII, v.1, an example  is given of the cruelty of Pilate to the Galileans, for, says the Evangelist, « there were present some that told him of the Galileans, whose blood Pilate had mingled with their sacrifices ». It would appear (see Josephus, XVIII, 4, 5) that Herod had taken upon himself to make anything but a favorable report of his colleague to Tiberias, speaking disparagingly of him both in public and in private, so that it is not much wonder that they were enemies. Herod Antipas, for it is of him we are now speaking, generally lived at his capital, Tiberias, but, on the occasion of the great festivals, he would naturally be at Jerusalem, and the probability is that he occupied the Palace of the Asmonians, situated on the left of the Temple at the foot of Mount Sion, or he may possibly have been staying in the Palace of his father, Herod the Great, which is situated a little farther to the west. In setting himself to curry favour with Herod, Pilate little expected how well he would succeed; the

JESUS BEFORE HEROD

tetrarch, blasé as he was from self-indulgence, anticipated a new pleasure in witnessing the marvellous works with which he hoped Jesus would entertain him. He no doubt took the Saviour for a kind of Simon the magician, who would be only too glad to win His liberty and the favour of the king by performing some wonderful feats of jugglery. Herod was very quickly undeceived, for, at the very first glance, the sight of the Nazarene must have affected him disagreeably; Jesus, it must be remembered, having been at the mercy of the populace since the morning. He had nothing on but His seamless garment, and He was in far too wretched and miserable a plight for His appearance to have given any pleasure to the effeminate sensualist, who delighted in the dancing of Salome and was given over to adultery. For all that, however, he received the Prisoner with a certain amount of empressement, overwhelming Him with a great flow of words and asking Him many questions, to all of which Jesus answered only with a silence full of majesty. It was a humiliating lesson for Herod; for this so-called King of the Jews seemed to take His title seriously and to look upon the tetrarch with absolute disdain. Herod was deeply wounded. The members of the Sanhedrim were there, vehemently accusing Jesus, and the bitterness of their rage against Him is expressed in the sacred text in a very striking manner : Stabant autem principes sacerdotum et scribæ constanter accusantes eum. Herod, though he does not believe all their angry accusations, means to have his revenge for the wound inflicted on his own self-love, and with this end in view he begins to set at naught and mock the Prisoner. This pretended King Who has been brought before him, is really too carelessly dressed. His royal purple is in too bad a condition, let us give Him a gorgeous robe more worthy of His sovereign dignity! Some old rags of white stuff are therefore hunted up from some neglected corner of the Palace, some comic-looking, tattered garment in which holes can easily be made for the head and arms, and behold there is Jesus arrayed in fitting guise for a pretender to the throne! A white garment (candidus) was in fact worn by candidates for a crown, and this garment resembled the gala dress of the wealthy and highly born. Thus arrayed, Jesus was sent back to Pilate before whom He had already been brought. Herod abandoning his rights.

Site of the Antonia Tower.

Certain rationalistic authors think the Gospel accounts of this scene are incorrect. They are of opinion that the insulting raillery of which Jesus was the object was the same as that referred to by Saint Matthew and Saint Mark and which, according to them, was levelled against Him not before Herod but in the Prætorium of the Roman Governor. To adopt the opinion of these authors could only lead to confusion. The suggestion they make is altogether gratuitous, for it is very evident that there were in reality two scenes when Christ was mocked: one referred to by Saint Luke only, the other by Saint Matthew and Saint Mark, but not by the other two Evangelists, so that instead of as alleged contradicting, the Gospel accounts supplement each other. This is the sort of thing which happens in so very many instances when prejudiced persons are anxious to detect inconsistencies.

Jesus led back from Herod to Pilate
Saint Luke – Chap. 23

T remisit (Jesum) ad Pilatum.

12. Et facti sunt amici Herodes et Pilatus in ipsa die; nam antea inimici erant ad invicem.

13. Pilatus autem, convocatis principibus sacerdotum et magistratibus et plebe,

14. Dixit ad illos : Obtulistis mihi hunc hominem quasi avertentem populum, et ecce ego coram vobis interrogans nullam causam inveni in homine isto ex his, in quibus eum accusatis.

15. Sed neque Herodes; nam remisi vos ad illum, et ecce nihil dignum morte actum est ei.

16. Emendatum ergo illum dimittam.

ND sent him again to Pilate.

12. And the same day Pilate and Herod were made friends together: for before they were at enmity between themselves.

13. And Pilate, when he had called together the chief priests and the rulers and the people,

Jesus led back from Herod to Pilate. J.-J. T.

14. Said unto them, Ye have brought this man unto me, as one that perverteth the people : and, behold, I, having examined *him* before you, have found no fault in this man touching those things whereof ye accuse him :

15. No, nor yet Herod : for I sent you to him ; and, lo, nothing worthy of death is done unto him.

16. I will therefore chastise him, and release *him*.

Pilate, warned of the return of Jesus, again appears upon the Judgment Seat to harangue the Jews and to tell them, no one contradicting him, that he has examined the accused and found Him innocent, thus convicting his hearers of hypocrisy and untruth. But in spite of all this the Governor's fear of the people makes him yield one iniquitous concession after another, until at last the death of the Just One is brought about. Already, although Pilate has « found no fault » in the Prisoner, he permits Him to be scourged.

EXPLANATORY NOTES

(1) Page 12: "If thou hadst known, even thou, at least in this thy day, the things which belong unto thy peace."

That is to say: If thou hadst known, in this day of pardon and salvation, when thy Saviour is with thee, that thy only chance of escaping from ruin and securing peace is by acknowledging Him as the Messiah, believing in His word and accepting His law. (Menochius, Fillion, etc.)

(2) Page 42: "They make broad their phylacteries."

The phylacteries were small strips of parchment on which were written certain passages from the Holy Scriptures; they were enclosed in little cases which the Jews wore fastened on their foreheads and on their arms by leather straps. (Calmet, Fillion, etc.)

(3) Page 51: "The abomination of desolation."

This abomination of desolation is differently explained by various commentators; it refers, perhaps, to the siege of Jerusalem by the idolatrous Romans, or, more probably still, to the desecration by the seditious Jews, who gave to themselves the name of Zealots, and who defiled the Temple with all manner of crimes a little before the taking of the town. (Cornel. a Lap., Maldonat, Fillion, etc.)

(4) Page 91: "He that hath seen me hath seen the Father."

Jesus here once more asserts His divinity; He and His Father are of one and the same nature; he who sees Him sees the same God as if he saw the Father Himself. (Cornelius a Lapide, Fillion, etc.)

LIST OF ILLUSTRATIONS

OF THE THIRD VOLUME

FULL-PAGE ILLUSTRATIONS

The first Denial of Saint Peter (Frontispiece)	Page
Our Lord Jesus Christ	88
Judas and with him a great multitude	98
The Bridge over the Brook Kedron	104
Christ mocked in the House of Caiaphas	116

ILLUSTRATIONS IN THE TEXT

The Foal of Bethphage	8
The Procession on the Mount of Olives	9
The Procession of the Apostles	10
"Jesus wept"	12
The Procession in the streets of Jerusalem	13
Yemenites of Jerusalem	15
The Multitude in the Temple	16
The Chief Priests take counsel together	17
Members of the Tribunal	18
The accursed Fig-tree	20
Christ driving out them that sold in the Temple	21
Jewish children	22
Jesus forbids the carrying of vessels through the Temple	24
The healing of the Lame in the Temple	25
Jesus goes out to Bethany in the evening	27
The Gentiles ask to see Jesus	29
Young girls of Bethlehem	31
The Voice from Heaven	32
The Chief Priests ask Jesus by whose authority He acts	33
The Corner Stone	36
The Tribute Money	37
Saint Luke	39
The Pharisees question Jesus	40
"Woe unto you, Scribes and Pharisees"	41
One of the Salome	42

LIST OF ILLUSTRATIONS

"Jerusalem, Jerusalem!"
The Widow's mite
A disciple from the South
The Disciples admire the buildings of the Temple
The Prophecy of the destruction of the Temple
Mary Magdalene's box of very precious ointment
The Jews conspire together
Exhortation to the Sinner
Judas goes to the Chief Priests
Christ going to the Mount of Olives at night
One of the Messengers of Saint John the Baptist
North-east angle of Jerusalem
Modern Jerusalem
Heathen Temple built by Hadrian on the site of Calvary
South-east angle of Jerusalem
The Man bearing a pitcher
Thursday evening
The Jews' Passover
The Lord's Supper: Judas dipping his hand in the dish
Jesus washing the Disciples' Feet
The Communion of the Apostles
Thursday evening
The Departure of Judas
The Last Discourse of Our Lord Jesus Christ
Women watching Jesus pass
Thursday evening
"Philip, he that hath seen me hath seen the Father"
The Protestations of Saint Peter
Saint Peter
"My soul is exceeding sorrowful unto death"
The Agony in the Garden
"Could ye not watch with me one hour?"
Judas
Thursday evening
Judas betraying Jesus with a kiss
"They went backward and fell to the ground"
Saint James the Less
Peter smites off the ear of Malchus
Christ healing the ear of Malchus
"And they all forsook him and fled"
Saint Peter and Saint John follow afar off
Thursday evening
Jesus taken before Annas
The false Witnesses before Caiaphas
The second Denial of Saint Peter
Annas and Caiaphas
The High Priest rends his clothes
Friday morning
"Jesus turned and looked upon Peter"

LIST OF ILLUSTRATIONS

	Page
"**Peter** went out and wept bitterly"	118
"The cock crew"	119
Friday morning	119
Friday **morning**: Jesus in prison	120
The Judgment on the morning of Good Friday	121
Judas repents and returns the price of blood	122
Friday morning	123
Judas hangs himself	124
The Apostles hiding in the Valley of Hinnom	125
Jesus led **from Caiaphas to Pilate**	128
Jesus before **Pilate** for the first time	129
Pilate	130
Friday morning	131
The Message **from Pilate's Wife**	132
Jesus **before Herod**	133
Jesus led back from Herod to Pilate	136

SUPPLEMENTARY ILLUSTRATIONS.

FAC-SIMILE WOOD ENGRAVINGS AFTER DRAWINGS

Capital from the El-Aksa Mosque	6
Path on the Mount of Olives	11
Out-buildings of the Armenian Convent at Jerusalem	14
Capital from the El-Aksa Mosque	14
A Fig-tree in the Valley of Hinnom	19
Women of Geba, Samaria	23
Path from Gethsemane to the Mount of the Ascension	26
A typical Jew of Jerusalem	28
Site of the Court of the Gentiles: Haram. Mount Zion in the distance	30
Esplanade of the Haram	34
An Armenian	35
Half-way up the Mount of Olives	38
A typical Jew	43
Steps in the Haram	47
A corner of the Haram, on the supposed site of the Temple	50
An Armenian	51
Transept of the El-Aksa Mosque	54
Antique frieze at Jelna on the road from Naplusium to Jerusalem	58
Pillar of a balustrade found in excavations at Jerusalem	62
Valley of Jehoshaphat, looking towards Shiloh	66
Antique cornice let into the wall of the Church of the Holy Sepulchre at Jerusalem	67
Capital from the El-Aksa Mosque	68
Walls of Jerusalem on the northern side	70
South-west angle of the Haram on the site of the Temple, taken from the Gate of the Mogarabies	71
The Tomb of Absalom in the Valley of Jehoshaphat	74

LIST OF ILLUSTRATIONS

Ornament in gilded metal from the Es-Sakhra Mosque, called the Mosque of Omar
Capital from the El-Aksa Mosque
Jerusalem as seen from the Hill of Evil Counsel
Ornament from the Valley of Hinnom
A typical Jew of Jerusalem
Ornament in gilded metal from the Es-Sakhra Mosque, called that of Omar
The Bridge of Kedron, coming from Gethsemane
The Valley of Jehoshaphat
Jerusalem from the south, with Sion and the Mosques of El-Aksa and of Omar on the left
The Bridge of Kedron and the Tomb of Absalom
The Valley of Jehoshaphat, coming from Bethany
The Valley of Hinnom (Aceldama)
Valley of Hinnom with its ancient tombs where the Apostles hid themselves
The greater part of the supposed site of the Temple
A corner of the Haram
Frieze from a Tomb of the Valley of Hinnom
Jerusalem and Shiloh
A typical Jew of Jerusalem
Site of the Antonia Tower

GENERAL INDEX OF THE CONTENTS

OF THE THIRD VOLUME

HOLY WEEK

	Page
Preface	5
The Foal of Bethphage	7
The Procession on the Mount of Olives	11
"Jesus wept"	12
The Procession in the Streets of Jerusalem	13
The Multitude in the Temple	15
The Chief Priests take Counsel together	17
The Accursed Fig-tree	19
Christ driving out them that sold in the Temple	21
Jesus forbids the carrying of vessels through the Temple	23
The Healing of the Lame in the Temple	24
Jesus goes out to Bethany in the evening	26
The Gentiles ask to see Jesus	28
The Voice from Heaven	30
The Chief Priests ask Jesus by whose authority He acts	33
The Corner Stone	35
The Tribute Money	37
The Pharisees question Jesus	39
"Woe unto you Scribes and Pharisees"	41
"Jerusalem! Jerusalem"	43
The Widow's Mite	45
The Disciples admire the Buildings of the Temple	47
The Prophecy of the Destruction of the Temple	49
Mary Magdalene's box of very precious ointment	51
The Jews conspire together	54
Judas goes to the Chief Priests	56
Christ going to the Mount of Olives at night	57
Explanatory Notes	59
List of Illustrations	61

THE PASSION

Introduction
Jerusalem
The Man bearing a Pitcher
The Jews' Passover
The Lord's Supper.—Judas dipping his hand in the dish
Jesus washing the Disciples' feet
The Communion of the Apostles
The Departure of Judas
The Last Discourse of Our Lord Jesus Christ
"Philip, he that hath seen me hath seen the Father"
The Protestations of Saint Peter
"My Soul is exceeding sorrowful unto death"
The Agony in the Garden
"Could ye not watch with me one hour?"
Judas and the Multitude with swords and staves
Judas betraying Jesus with a kiss
"They went backward and fell to the ground"
Peter smites off the ear of Malchus
Christ healing the ear of Malchus
De Torrente in via bibet
"And they all forsook him and fled"
Saint Peter and Saint John follow afar off
The Via Dolorosa
Jesus taken before Annas
The False Witnesses before Caiaphas
Saint Peter and Saint John enter the Court
The second Denial of Saint Peter
The High Priest rends his clothes
"The Lord turned and looked upon Peter"
Christ buffeted and mocked in the House of Caiaphas
"The cock crew"
"Peter went out and wept bitterly"
Good Friday.—The morning: Jesus in prison
The Judgment on the morning of Good Friday
Judas repents and returns the price of blood
Judas hangs himself
The Apostles hiding in the Valley of Hinnom
Jesus led from Caiaphas to Pilate
Jesus before Pilate for the first time
The Message from Pilate's Wife
Jesus before Herod
Jesus led back from Herod to Pilate

www.ingramcontent.com/pod-product-compliance
Lightning Source LLC
Chambersburg PA
CBHW030350170426
43202CB00010B/1326